David, who made this book possible.

NUMBERED ROUTES

1. Lilongwe - Kasungu **(M1)**
2. Kasungu - Kasungu National Park/Lifupa Camp **(S55)**
3. Kasungu - Kamuzu Academy - Nkhotakota **(S54/M10)**
4. Kasungu - Mzuzu **(M1)**
5. Mzuzu - Nkhata Bay **(M12)** - Chintheche - Dwangwa - Nkhotakota **(S53)**
6. Mzuzu - Rumphi turnoff **(M1)**
7. **M1/S85** junction - Rumphi **(S85)** - Chelinda Camp, Nyika National Park **(S10)**
8. Rumphi junction - Livingstonia - Chitimba **(S86)**
9. Rumphi turnoff - Chitimba **(M1)**
10. Chitimba - Chilumba jetty - Karonga **(M1, S76)**
11. Lilongwe - Livingstonia Beach (via Salima) **(M5)**
12. Salima - Nkhotakota **(M5/S33)**
13. Salima - Balaka **(M17/M1)**
14. Mua - Lakeshore Road, south of Monkey Bay **(M18)**
15. Junction of M18 with Monkey Bay/Mangochi Road - Monkey Bay **(M15)**
16. Junction of M18 with Monkey Bay/Mangochi Road - Mangochi **(M15)**
17. Mangochi - M1 junction near Liwonde **(M3)**
18. Lilongwe - Blantyre **(M1/M2)**
19. Balaka (via Liwonde) - Zomba **(M1)**
20. Zomba - Blantyre **(M1)**
21. Blantyre - Thyolo - Mulanje **(M1)**
22. Blantyre - Chikwawa - Nsanje **(S38)**

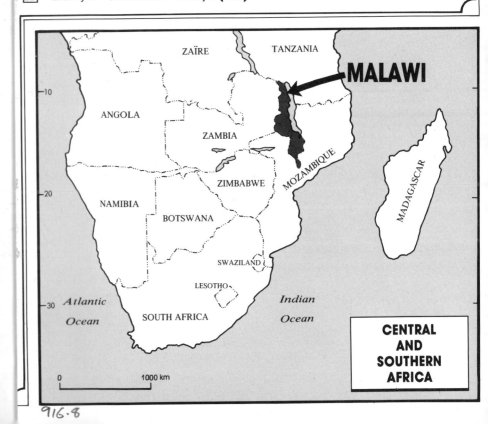

CENTRAL AND SOUTHERN AFRICA

Ma

Fo

Visitors'
Guide to

Malawi

How to get there
What to see
Where to stay

Martine Maurel

SOUTHERN
BOOK PUBLISHERS

ISBN 1 86812 283 2

First edition, first impression 1990

Published by
Southern Book Publishers (Pty) Ltd
P.O. Box 548, Bergvlei 2012
Johannesburg

Cover photograph by Mike Schulze
Cover design by Insight Graphics
Set in 10 on 11½ pt Palatino
by Kohler Carton & Print, Natal
Printed and bound by Kohler Carton & Print, Natal

AUTHOR'S NOTE

It is wise to regard maps supplied in this book as guidelines only as the conditions of roads change markedly over time and with the seasons. Rampant growth of vegetation, detours caused by excessive rain damage and lack of use are all factors which may lead to the creation of new roads and abandonment of old roads.

Before embarking on any journey, the visitor would be well advised to check routes with the Department of Tourism in Blantyre, Map Sales Offices, Department of Surveys either in Lilongwe or Blantyre, and Department of National Parks and Wildlife either in Lilongwe or Blantyre.

PREFACE

This book could be said to be written on the horns of a dilemma. One horn urges that Malawi be written about: a country with so much inherent beauty should be enjoyed and appreciated by more people. The other horn urges one to keep one's mouth closed and hug the secret of Malawi to oneself lest she does get put on the international tourist map in a big way.

Suffice it to say that Malawi really does deserve to be written about. The reader will know what is meant only when he or she has visited this very special place, which together with its very special people, tends to leave its imprint on one's soul.

A number of books about Malawi have been published but most are either out of date, out of print or difficult to obtain. Some of those that are available are specialised in terms of subject matter, thus presenting a practical problem for the casual tourist who would normally not have the time to sift through a variety of different sources of information.

Visitors' Guide to Malawi attempts to overcome this problem by covering information found in most of these sources and offering the tourist general information to answer any immediate questions. A list of books that would satisfy more specialist information requirements is printed at the back of the book.

CONTENTS

6. FACTORS AFFECTING YOUR PLANNING

7. WHERE TO STAY

8. MISCELLANEOUS INFORMATION

INTRODUCTION

The four corners of Malawi are accessible by various means for those keen to undertake mildly challenging overland travels while savouring Africa's spellbinding wilderness. At the same time, those who wish to escape from the rat race to what amounts to the proverbial tropical paradise will find plenty of opportunity to put their feet up while basking peacefully in the sun on Lake Malawi's golden shores.

It is not lightly that the sobriquet "The warm heart of Africa" is used to describe Malawi. Lying within the tropics and stretching from her most northerly point just 9° 45′ south of the equator to 17° 16′ south, Malawi offers the visitor all the climatic delights pulsating from Africa's heart. Not only is the climate warm – Malawi's people are some of the warmest on the continent. They are unerringly polite, pleasant and gentle people who contribute to making a visit to Malawi so much more memorable.

In the realm of wildlife, elephant, hippo and crocodile abound, as do antelope, hyena, monkeys and baboons, while leopards are no strangers to the northern region of the country. For those with special interests, Malawi's birds and orchids have much to offer and are well catalogued to assist the explorer in finding and identifying them.

Those who simply enjoy scenic beauty will find Malawi richly endowed for such a small country. Travel from one place to another is never boring: there is always some different and striking human, topographic or vegetative feature to capture one's interest.

But these are all mere jewels in Malawi's crown, the stunning centrepiece of which is her lake. Stretching north to south (in miles) for as long as there are days in the year and east to west as wide as there are weeks in the year, Lake Malawi offers one the opportunity to forget about the hurried passing of time. Still relatively untouched by the modern world, the lake is a vast embodiment of a thousand picture postcards.

HOW TO USE THIS GUIDE

Chapter 1 offers some background on Malawi's history and the forces that have shaped her into what she is today.

Having gained a broad perspective, consult Chapter 2, which should help you decide on the places you would like to visit, taking into account your possible special interests (Chapter 3).

Once you know where to go, read Chapter 4, which will tell you how to get to Malawi, either by road or by air, and what formalities and practical considerations will apply once you enter the country.

Chapter 5 explains the different methods of travel available in Malawi and also provides a description of the standard routes you might take to get from place to place.

Chapter 6 gives information on certain factors that may affect the timing of your visit, how to avoid illness and what to do if it does strike, and items you might consider bringing into the country to make your visit more pleasurable.

Having decided which areas you wish to visit, how to get there and what you would like to do during your stay, consult Chapter 7 to plan your accommodation.

Finally, Chapter 8 contains miscellaneous information that may come in handy when you plan your trip or while you are in Malawi.

1 THE FACTORS THAT SHAPE MALAWI

GEOGRAPHY

Malawi is one of the smaller African nations. Situated between 9° and 18° south of the equator and between 33° and 36° east, it could be described as forming part of Southern Central Africa. Its neighbours include Zambia to the west, Tanzania to the north and north-east and Mozambique to the south-west, south and east.

Malawi is a narrow country some 900 km long and between 80 and 160 km wide. All in all it covers an area of over 118 000 km², whose dominant feature is an enormous lake, officially classified as an inland sea. The third largest lake in Africa and ranking twelfth in size in world terms, Lake Malawi lies in the deep trough in the earth's surface formed by the southern portion of the African Rift Valley as it runs through Malawi from north to south.

Central Africa's highest mountain, Mulanje (3 002 m), lies in the south-eastern corner of Malawi. After Mulanje, other high-lying areas in Malawi include the Zomba Plateau (2 133 m) in the south, the Nyika Plateau (2 600 m) in the north and the lower-lying Dedza and Viphya plateaux. At the opposite end of the spectrum is the hot and humid lower Shire Valley, which at its lowest point is only 37 m above sea-level.

Malawi's lake and varied altitudes influence the country's tropical continental climate, which comprises three main seasons: the hot-wet (November to April), cool-dry (May to August) and hot-dry seasons (September to November). Temperatures range from freezing at the highest altitudes in the winter months to 38° C at the lowest altitude in the summer months. The wet season generally lasts from November to May and rainfall varies countrywide from 600 mm to 3 000 mm.

HISTORY

Stone Age evidence dating back to 10 000 BC has led theorists to believe that pygmy bushmen were Malawi's first inhabitants. These were followed by migrating Bantu from Angola in the east at around AD 1300.

By the fifteenth century Arabs and Portuguese had visited the area, which was then dominated by the Maravi people from whom the country derives its modern name. Arab slave trading had become well established in the region by 1870, so much so that at least 20 000 slaves were being handled every year.

David Livingstone, the famous Scottish explorer, visited the country in 1859 and named the lake Lake Nyasa. His visits to the region resulted in an influx of British missionaries. These were soon followed by settlers keen to further British imperial and commercial interests, a drive which led to the declaration of Nyasaland (as it was then known) in 1891 as a British protectorate.

A federation of Northern and Southern Rhodesia (now Zambia and Zimbabwe) and Nyasaland was formed under British rule in 1953 despite growing African opposition to continued colonial domination. The federation was short-lived, however, as Dr Hastings Kamuzu Banda (now Malawi's Life President) returned to his country from self-exile in Britain in 1958 demanding independence from colonial rule. This was granted in 1964 and Nyasaland became known as Malawi. Two years later, Malawi became a republic within the Commonwealth group of nations.

In 1989 Malawi celebrated 25 years of independence. In that time it has been ruled by an elected parliament headed by His Excellency, Dr H. Kamuzu Banda and has enjoyed much stability and growth, qualities that have been denied to many other African countries. Under Dr Banda, Malawi has become a peaceful nation of God-fearing and law-abiding citizens dedicated to the goal of agricultural self-sufficiency. In comparison with colonial times, much has been done to improve the country's infrastructure and great emphasis has been put on the improvement of educational facilities.

Malawi is a one-party state and the Malawi Congress Party is its national party.

ECONOMY

A mixed economy approach has been followed since independence but the economy's major emphasis, to date, has focused on the agricultural sector. Malawi's wide-ranging climatic conditions have facilitated the development of such tropical and subtropical crops as maize, tobacco, sugar, cotton, groundnuts, timber, tea, coffee and rubber. The main export crops are sugar, tea and tobacco. Another major earner of foreign exchange is tourism.

POPULATION

With just under a quarter of its total land area taken up by its lakes, Malawi is one of the most densely populated countries in Africa. To give a more graphic idea of this fact, Malawi should be compared with neighbouring Zambia, which is much larger in size but has less than Malawi's seven million population (estimated in 1984).

Unlike many other African countries, it is difficult to travel any distance without seeing some evidence of human habitation. Only one per cent of the population is non-African and this group, which is mainly made up of Asians and Europeans, resides in the larger urban areas of Blantyre, Lilongwe and Zomba. Blantyre has by far the largest population of any urban centre in Malawi.

2 WHERE TO GO

The name "Malawi" means "reflected light" or "bright haze", words that aptly describe what Malawi is all about. They evoke the warm hospitality of the Malawian people, who are always friendly and welcoming; they describe the golden light suffusing the still waters of the lake at sunrise and sunset. Not least, the words describe the kindness of the climate.

Malawi offers paradise to the watersport enthusiast as well as a haven to the lover of wildlife who wishes to wander freely in the deceptive quiet of the bush.

The visitor who yearns to rejoin civilisation for a day or two can enjoy a first-class meal in one of Malawi's cities or spend a kwacha or two shopping for curios as well as everyday items, most of which are available in the well-stocked shops.

THE MAIN CENTRES

Lilongwe

The split-personality city of Lilongwe was named after the river that rises nearby in the Dzalanyama ("full of animals") Hills and meanders across the plain through the city to join the Linthipe River on its lake-ward-bound journey.

At an elevation of 1 000 m above sea-level, Lilongwe is conveniently situated at the crossroads of Malawi's road and rail network, which links the city with Blantyre to the south, Salima and the lake to the east, the Zambian border and Lusaka to the west, Kasungu, Mzuzu, the Nyika Plateau and national park, and ultimately Tanzania to the north.

The modern Kamuzu International Airport lies 26 km to the north of the city and has taken over from the old Chileka Airport in Blantyre as Malawi's international airport.

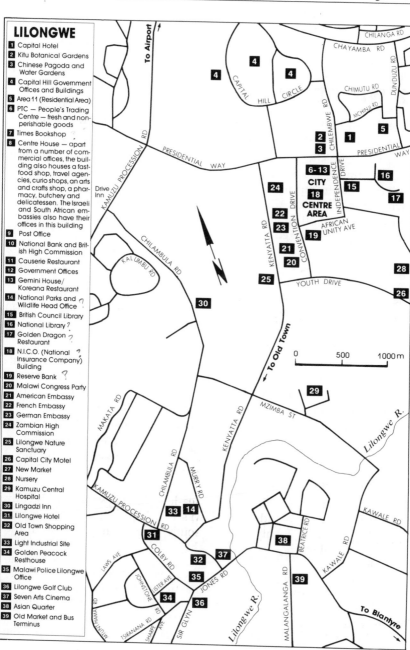

LILONGWE

1. Capital Hotel
2. Kitu Botanical Gardens
3. Chinese Pagoda and Water Gardens
4. Capital Hill Government Offices and Buildings
5. Area 11 (Residential Area)
6. PTC — People's Trading Centre — fresh and non-perishable goods
7. Times Bookshop
8. Centre House — apart from a number of commercial offices, the building also houses a fast-food shop, travel agencies, curio shops, an arts and crafts shop, a pharmacy, butchery and delicatessen. The Israeli and South African embassies also have their offices in this building
9. Post Office
10. National Bank and British High Commission
11. Causerie Restaurant
12. Government Offices
13. Gemini House/Koreana Restaurant
14. National Parks and Wildlife Head Office
15. British Council Library
16. National Library
17. Golden Dragon Restaurant
18. N.I.C.O. (National Insurance Company) Building
19. Reserve Bank
20. Malawi Congress Party
21. American Embassy
22. French Embassy
23. German Embassy
24. Zambian High Commission
25. Lilongwe Nature Sanctuary
26. Capital City Motel
27. New Market
28. Nursery
29. Kamuzu Central Hospital
30. Lingadzi Inn
31. Lilongwe Hotel
32. Old Town Shopping Area
33. Light Industrial Site
34. Golden Peacock Resthouse
35. Malawi Police Lilongwe Office
36. Lilongwe Golf Club
37. Seven Arts Cinema
38. Asian Quarter
39. Old Market and Bus Terminus

Officially named as the new capital of Malawi in 1975, the fledgeling city is known as both the "Capital City" and the "Garden City". Although its history stretches back into the earlier reaches of the century, it is only in the last two decades that it has started being developed as a modern city, hence its division into "Old Town" and "New Town".

Soon after the turn of the century a local chief, Njawa, requested of the British Protectorate administration that a new *boma* or administrative section be established in the area of present-day Lilongwe.

The administration saw the value of the site as a more practical administrative headquarters for the Central Region and its representatives set up camp in 1902 on the west bank of the Lilongwe River, where the offices of Admarc stand today. By 1905, the settlement had a population of 30 and a new trunk road measuring approximately five metres in width linked it with Dedza in the south.

The eastern bank of the river, which previously formed part of a game reserve, was rezoned in 1906 to allow the settlement of the first Asian traders. Mandala (the African Lakes Company) and what is known as Kandodo today were two of the first companies to establish their offices in this area. By 1909, communication with the outside world had been eased by a trunk road built to link Lilongwe with Zambia via Mchinji in the west.

In 1922, an African hospital was built in the grounds of the present-day Lilongwe Golf Club, whose clubhouse was built in 1932 after the hospital was resited. Lilongwe's first hotel was built in 1929 and by 1932 the Asian community had expanded to the extent that it had established its own mosque, sports club and at least 20 trading stores.

In 1947, in confirmation of Lilongwe's importance as a communication centre for Malawi's trade routes, the settlement was accorded township status.

Its original population of 30 having grown to 20 000, Lilongwe became a municipality in 1966. The move to make it the capital city started in 1968 as the result of the need to direct development away from the more densely populated Southern Region to the economically neglected Central and Northern regions.

The idea of forming a new capital city was conceived by His Excellency, the Life President, Dr H. Kamuzu Banda while in detention in Gwelo Prison in Southern Rhodesia during the late 1950s. Lilongwe, as the second largest urban centre, was the logical site. It was reasoned that the entire country could be more practically administered from

Lilongwe and that new investment in the area would stimulate agriculture and industry, while providing much-needed employment. Moreover, government offices, until then housed in ageing buildings in Zomba, were rapidly expanding and needed the cohesion and space that would be supplied by a new capital.

Capital Hill, which today houses the government administration offices and forms the nucleus of the Capital City, was hewn out of virgin forest. Town planning authorities have very sensibly kept the Capital City's origins very much in mind when planning road grids and building layouts and in so doing, have ensured that nature has remained a bold feature of the city.

The visitor will notice the very carefully tended public gardens which boast a wide array of brilliantly coloured tropical blooms and plants. During the March/April period, a particularly lovely sight is the rows of yellow acacia trees that line many of the capital's roadways. In the winter months of May, June and July the bright red of the poinsettia adds splashes of colour to the landscape, giving way to the lilac splendour of the jacarandas until December when the flame trees burst into bloom.

A guide to Lilongwe (numbers refer to map on page 7)

1 Capital Hotel
2 Kitu Botanical Gardens
3 Chinese pagoda and water gardens
4 Capital Hill government offices and buildings
5 Area 11 (residential area)
6 Area 12 (residential area)
7 PTC – People's Trading Centre – fresh and non-perishable goods
8 Times Bookshop
9 Centre House – Apart from a number of commercial offices, the building also houses a fast-food shop, travel agencies, curio shops, an arts and crafts shop, a pharmacy, butchery and delicatessen. The Israeli and South African embassies have their offices here
10 Post Office
11 National Bank and British High Commission
12 Causerie Restaurant
13 Government offices
14 Gemini House/ Koreana Restaurant
15 British Council and Library
16 National Parks and Wildlife Head Office

17 National Library ?
18 Golden Dragon Restaurant ?
19 N.I.C.O. (National Insurance Company) building ?
20 Commercial Bank
21 Reserve Bank
22 Malawi Congress Party
23 American Embassy
24 French Embassy
25 German Embassy
26 Zambian High Commission
27 Lilongwe Nature Sanctuary
28 Capital City Motel
29 New Market
30 Nursery
31 Kamuzu Central Hospital
32 Lingadzi Inn
33 Lilongwe Hotel
34 Old Town shopping area
35 Light industrial site
36 Area 3 (residential area)
37 Area 9 (residential area)
38 Golden Peacock Resthouse
39 Malawi Police Lilongwe office
40 Seven Arts Cinema
41 Asian quarter
42 Old market and bus terminus

Note: Not all the residential areas have been listed as it is assumed the tourist is more likely to need to know where places of interest are situated.

The Lilongwe Nature Sanctuary

Centrally situated between Old and New towns, the Nature Sanctuary comprises 120 hectares of land adjacent to the Lingadzi River that can be toured by following paths on foot.

Wildlife in the sanctuary includes many small animals such as porcupine, civet, serval, genet, vervet monkeys, bushbabies, squirrels, duiker, and bushpig, as well as larger game such as bushbuck, leopard, and hyena.

Some of the most interesting of the many species of bird to be seen in the sanctuary are the red-winged warbler, the pied mannikin, African broadbill, giant eagle owl, green loerie and African paradise flycatcher. The river is home to crocodiles, otters and 14 species of fish.

It should not be assumed that the sanctuary is similar to a city zoo, just because it is situated near the city. The sanctuary was established in order to give the visitor an idea of the fauna and flora that existed in the area before construction began. The walk is undertaken without a guide so you should be as alert as you would be in the bush. In the fairly recent past, leopards have been seen crossing the road just outside the sanctuary at night, so they too are in the vicinity. The presence of hyena should also not be discounted.

The Asian quarter

Across the river from Old Town is a motley collection of old single storey buildings, lining the road on both sides, which houses the Asian commercial quarter. In marked contrast to the order and relative calm of New Town, many colourful characters ply their trade in the quarter, giving the area a lively, bustling air.

On the verandas of the buildings sit numerous tailors ready to tackle any item of clothing from a simple repair to a cocktail garment and all for a very reasonable rate. Short of space to display the fruits of their abilities, the tailors adorn shop railings with brightly coloured dresses that have cardboard strategically inserted in such a manner that allows no guessing as to the gender of the potential wearer of the garment!

While in the quarter you will also hear the amplified sounds of the muezzin emitting from the mosque calling the faithful to prayer.

The old market

A must for every tourist is the Lilongwe market in Malangalanga Road. The market can be reached by taking the first turning to the right off Sir Glyn Jones Road after crossing the bridge.

In it you can buy fruit and vegetables in season, dried fish (which accounts for the rather rich odour pervading the air), live chickens for the pot, basketware, tin lamps fashioned to look like aeroplanes, fresh meat, even ball bearings, nails and screws, which almost unbelievably are sold singly.

You can even buy odd hardware from the hardware section in the market or have a dustbin, watering-can or cooking pot made by the tinkers on the spot. These account for the loud tapping noise you hear on entering the market.

Although meat is sold at the market, it is advisable to purchase meat from the PTC (People's Trading Centre) supermarket, which has a superior standard of hygiene but which is correspondingly more expensive.

The fruit and vegetable section of the market usually has a fair selection of items for sale. The worst time of the year for purchasing fruit and vegetables is during and just after the wet season, when the price of tomatoes is exorbitant. Between February and May, onions, tomatoes and carrots are not abundantly available, nor is their quality particularly good (see page 180/181 for a list detailing availability of fruit and vegetables).

However, at other times of the year, for example closer to June, the visitor to the market may spy a huge mound of tangerines or oranges being sold for just a few tambala each.

Remember to bargain when in the market (see Notes on bargaining, page 92) for if you are obviously a tourist, prices charged can be quite unrealistic.

If you want to take photographs in the market – or, indeed, anywhere – have the courtesy to ask permission first, otherwise you risk offending someone's dignity.

Blantyre

Named after the birthplace of the great African explorer, Dr David Livingstone, in Scotland, Blantyre began existence as a mission site on 23 October 1876 when it was founded by the missionaries of the Established Church of Scotland.

The missionaries had originally chosen Zomba as the site for their mission but later decided that it was too close to the slave-trade routes as well as being a haven for dangerous wild animals. In their search for an alternative, safer, site they were led to Blantyre by one of their guides, who originally came from the district.

Blantyre was also perceived to be a convenient centre for communication and travel links between the lower Shire Valley and the port of Quelimane in Mozambique and the upper Shire and the lake.

Blantyre's situation in the heart of the agriculturally rich Shire Highlands, which because of their higher altitude offered a more temperate climate than the hot and humid Shire Valley, made it attractive to the first commercial settlers who followed the missionaries after a few years. Blantyre soon became the centre of trade for the region, which resulted in it becoming Malawi's most densely populated region. Malawi's first

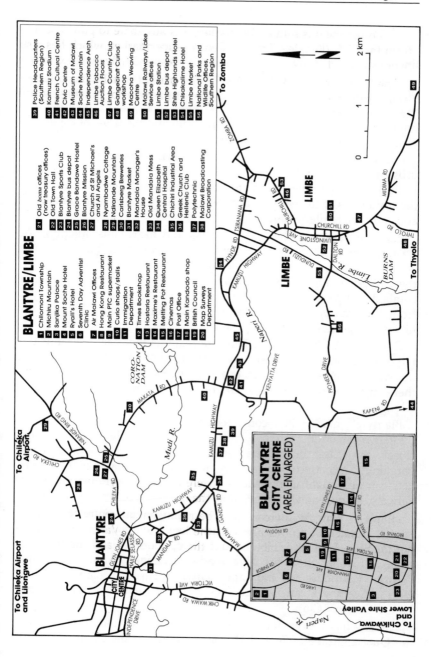

BLANTYRE/LIMBE

1 Chilomoni Township
2 Michiru Mountain
3 Sanjika Palace
4 Mount Soche Hotel
5 Ryall's Hotel
6 Seventh Day Adventist Clinic
7 Air Malawi Offices
8 Hong Kong Restaurant
9 Main PTC supermarket
10 Curio shops/stalls
11 Immigration Department
12 Times Bookshop
13 Hostaria Restaurant
14 Maxime's Restaurant
15 Melting Pot Restaurant
16 Cinemas
17 Post Office
18 Main Kandodo shop
19 British Council
20 Map Surveys Department

21 Old *boma* offices (now treasury offices)
22 Old Town Hall
23 Blantyre Sports Club
24 Blantyre bus depot
25 Grace Bandawe Hostel
26 Blantyre Mission
27 Church of St Michael's and All Angels
28 Nyambadwe Cottage
29 Ndirande Mountain
30 Carlsberg Breweries
31 Blantyre Market
32 Mandala Manager's House
33 Old Mandala Mess
34 Queen Elizabeth Central Hospital
35 Chichiri Industrial Area
36 Greek Church and Hellenic Club
37 Polytechnic
38 Malawi Broadcasting Corporation

39 Police Headquarters (Southern Region)
40 Kamuzu Stadium
41 French Cultural Centre
42 Civic Centre
43 Museum of Malawi
44 Soche Mountain
45 Independence Arch
46 Limbe Tobacco Auction Floors
47 Limbe Country Club
48 Gangecraft Curios workshop
49 Macoha Weaving Centre
50 Malawi Railways/Lake Service offices
51 Limbe Station
52 Limbe bus depot
53 Shire Highlands Hotel
54 Chisakalime Hotel
55 Limbe Market
56 National Parks and Wildlife Offices, Southern Region

airport was built at Chileka, 19 km outside Blantyre, and this served to reinforce its position as the centre of commerce and industry, a distinction it retains today.

With its infrastructure adequately established and a population rapidly growing out of proportion to available resources, it was decided that the focus of activity should be shifted away from Blantyre to Lilongwe, where a new capital was being built and the fruits of expansion could be more profitably savoured.

Central Africa's oldest municipality comprises the neighbouring suburbs of Blantyre and Limbe, which are joined by 8 km of highway. With its more European climate, Limbe was favoured as the site for the residences of the early settlers, while Blantyre attracted commercial and industrial enterprises.

Blantyre nestles in the midst of hills and mountains: Michiru, the "rain mountain", above Chilomoni township; craggy Chiradzulu, which is off the Zomba road; Ndirande, the "sleeping man mountain", off the Chileka road, and Soche Mountain. These mountains can all be climbed and panoramic views of the city and environs can be enjoyed from their summits (see section entitled "For walkers, climbers and hikers", page 64).

Compared with Lilongwe, Blantyre really is the "big city", but this tag doesn't mean it has lost its village character. It offers far more in the way of shopping as far as everyday items are concerned although there may not be as great a variety of curios as are to be found in Lilongwe.

Blantyre's market is a concrete affair with not half the charm of Lilongwe's market. Perhaps Limbe's market resembles the latter more closely but it is a bit off the beaten track. If you prefer to give the bargaining and atmosphere a miss, most things available at these markets can be bought in the shops at reasonable prices, except for basketware, second-hand clothing and various items of wooden furniture.

Hotels in Blantyre include the top-quality Mount Soche Hotel and Ryall's Hotel, just around the corner from one another, while Limbe has the Shire Highlands Hotel and the Hotel Chisakalime. For the lower budget traveller there are Nyambadwe Cottage, Namiwawa Lodge, Blantyre Resthouse and the Grace Bandawe Hostel in Blantyre. Those who are camping can use facilities at the Blantyre Sports Club and Limbe Country Club.

The city has a large, fairly modern, government-controlled hospital, the Queen Elizabeth Central Hospital, as well as the smaller Seventh

Day Adventist Clinic run privately by American missionaries. There are also a number of doctors in private practice.

Blantyre's situation offers easy motoring access to a number of interesting places, all within a few hours' drive along good tarred roads. These include Zomba (59 km), Thyolo's lush tea-growing estates (39 km), Mulanje (66 km), the Mfunda Falls at Matope (60 km), Mpatamanga Gorge on the Chileka road (53 km), Lengwe National Park in Chikwawa District (73 km) and the Mangochi lakeshore (185 km via Zomba).

Blantyre's main shopping area takes the form of a triangle bordered by Victoria Avenue, Haile Selassie Road and Glyn Jones Road. The entire triangle can easily be toured on foot in about an hour, depending on your inclination to stop and shop.

Down Victoria Avenue and heading towards the Old Town Hall are a number of shops and banks including a pharmacy, the main PTC supermarket, the British Council Library, a curio shop, a crafts shop and a bookshop. A number of travel agencies with offices face the road and further down Victoria Avenue is another large supermarket, which offers more or less the same items for sale as the large PTC. Visitors can extend their permits at the Immigration Department in Building Society House, which is on the corner opposite the PTC.

Outside the large PTC facing a side road is a covered section specially built as a venue for the sale of Malawian curios. Prices here are open to negotiation while across the road at the Gangecraft shop, prices are fixed.

At the bottom of Victoria Avenue is a collection of ageing buildings which used to form the town's *boma* during colonial times. Still standing are the Old Town Hall, built in 1903 to celebrate the reign of Queen Victoria, after whom the main avenue was named, the Old Library, which now contains private offices, and the tax and treasury departments, which still operate as such today. The buildings have been listed as national monuments. Maps of Malawi are sold at the Map Surveys Department just a few metres away from the Old Town Hall (see address on page 184).

The bulk of the city's main administrative functions are now carried out from the recently built Civic Centre buildings, which are visible from the roundabout just past the Kamuzu Stadium in the suburb of Chichiri.

A little beyond the Old Library, following the turn-off to the right, is the Blantyre Sports Club, which like the Lilongwe Golf Club offers a range of sporting and camping facilities that are available on payment of a temporary membership fee. Visiting members of other Central and Southern African clubs are granted temporary membership on a reciprocal basis. Club facilities include The Copper Bowl restaurant, which has a good reputation.

The shops along Haile Selassie Road are mostly run by Asian entrepreneurs whose front verandas house the ubiquitous tailors and watchrepairers. With names like "Silky Touch Hairdressing", "Fit-o-fit tailors"and "Bombay Bazaars" the shops, in themselves, are also interesting to visit, for in them you can buy anything from a paperclip to a mosquito net.

The area forming the interior of the triangle contains a wide assortment of shops and offices, including The Hostaria, an Italian restaurant, Maxim's Restaurant and a pair of modern cinemas. Worth visiting too is the Central Bookshop with its relatively large selection of specialist publications concerning Malawi.

At the roundabout Haile Selassie Road meets with Glyn Jones Road, which leads back to the Mount Soche Hotel. Among other shops and boutiques, there are two curio shops along this road that may be of interest to the visitor. The main post office is also situated here.

Continuing on Glyn Jones Road past the Mount Soche, at the first turning to the right into Robins Road are the Air Malawi offices on the right, the Hong Kong restaurant on the left and past that, the Seventh Day Adventist Clinic, which offers a number of medical and dental services to the public.

Places of interest between Blantyre and Limbe along Kamuzu Highway, which links the two areas, include the Greek church of St Nektarios and the Hellenic Club.

The Queen Elizabeth Central Hospital is reached by taking the righthand turn at the first set of traffic lights on Kamuzu Highway and immediately thereafter turning left. The hospital is clearly signposted.

Continuing along Kamuzu Highway are the offices of the Polytechnic and School of Accountancy on the right, an area which is also to be the site of the new Medical School and School of Nursing. These are all constituent colleges of the University of Malawi, which has its main campus in Zomba. The gradual development of the University since Malawi attained her independence over a quarter of a century ago is the fulfilment of another of the goals that the Life President nurtured while imprisoned in Southern Rhodesia.

The orderly layout of the buildings lining Kamuzu Highway at this point belies the existence of a bustling industrial area, Chichiri, to the rear of the highway. The suburb houses the bulk of Malawi's industrial infrastructure.

Further along on the right-hand side and set well back from the road are the High Court of Malawi, Malawi Broadcasting Corporation offices and Police Headquarters for the Southern Region. On the opposite side of the road lie the showgrounds, the site of international and local trade fairs. The imposing Kamuzu Stadium, which is on the left just before the roundabout, is the gathering place of thousands during Independence Day Celebrations (6 July) as well as a number of nationally important events that are all celebrated with traditional dancing by the colourfully dressed *mbumba* (female dancers), speeches, parades and displays. It is also the setting for the very popular local and international football matches.

To the right of the roundabout a road almost immediately to the left leads to the French Cultural Centre on the right, the modern offices of the Civic Centre on the left (visible from Kamuzu Highway), and the small but interesting Museum of Malawi further along on the left.

To reach Limbe, continue along Kamuzu Highway under the Independence Arch and keep to the right when the road forks a little further on. The road bearing to the left leads to Zomba and the Central and Northern regions. Just a little way up the road on the left is the medium-priced Hotel Chisakalime, which has a very popular nightclub.

Limbe contains an abundance of small Asian shops, most selling clothing materials and hardware items. It is also the site of the Limbe Tobacco Auction floors, the Shire Highlands Hotel, the headquarters of Lonrho (Malawi), Malawi Railway Headquarters and the Limbe Club – which, like the Blantyre and Lilongwe clubs, offers the visitor access to a number of sporting and entertainment facilities on a daily membership basis. As with the Blantyre Club, arrangements can be made for reciprocal temporary membership for visitors who are also members of clubs in the Central and Southern African region.

To reach the tea-growing estates of Thyolo and ultimately Mulanje, take the right-hand fork just past the Limbe Club, which is on the left of Churchill Road. This double-laned road eventually becomes a single-strip tar road and passes the turn-off for Gangecraft Curios workshop, which is open to the public from Mondays to Saturdays. Here you can purchase a wide range of wooden Malawian curios which are made on the premises by craftsmen. Gangecraft prices are not subject to negotiation. It's worth asking the supervisor on duty to take you on a conducted tour of the workshops. You'll see the wood being sawn before it is handed to the craftsmen for carving.

Instead of bearing to the right at the fork, the visitor can continue along Churchill Road, which becomes Midima Road and leads to the Macoha Weaving Centre. The workshop is clearly signposted on the right-hand side of the road. It is worth visiting this hive of activity where blind people busily weave a variety of cotton mats, hammocks, carpets, ethnic wallhangings, bags and oven gloves. These reasonably priced items are on sale in the centre's shop and they can also be ordered to individual specification (though you should expect a certain amount of delay in receiving the finished article).

Some other places of interest in and around Blantyre that are worth visiting include the following:

The Church of St Michael's and All Angels CCAP (Church of Central Africa Presbyterian), which is to be found set back to the left of the Chileka road as you head out of the city. It forms the nucleus of the Blantyre Mission complex, the first form of continuous European settlement in the country. The church was built between 1888 and 1891 by a missionary, the Reverend Clement Scott, who had been completely untutored in the discipline of architecture and relied wholly on his common sense when designing and building the church.

Still in daily use, the church was the first permanent place of Christian worship in Central Africa. It is also a protected monument.

The Catholic Church of St Montfort, built in 1914, is reached via Victoria Avenue, turning right at the T-junction with Mahatma Gandhi Road. Just before the junction with the Chikwawa road, the church is set on the right-hand side on a rather neglected piece of land. Opposite is the Archbishop's residence, where Pope John Paul II stayed during his visit to Malawi in 1989.

To reach the *original commercial section of Blantyre*, take Mandala Road, which leads off Haile Selassie Road, and continue across the bridge and up the hill. On the left-hand side before the summit of the hill is the Mandala Manager's House. Completed in 1882, it formed the original company headquarters of the African Lakes Company, which began the first commercial trading activities in Malawi. Today, the interior of the house has been renovated to house modern offices, but members of the public are still welcome to visit.

It is interesting to note that the name "Mandala", meaning "reflected pools" in Chichewa, was the nickname given to the bespectacled John

Moir, who, together with his brother Frederick Moir, was the first manager of the company. Eventually the company came to be known as "Mandala".

Further up the road in what is known as "top Mandala", on the right-hand side of the road, set back in a hedged area is the Old Mandala Mess, which formed the living quarters of the African Lakes Company staff. Nowadays, the two-storey building, with its wide verandas, serves as the headquarters of the Malawi Museum Service.

Blantyre Market is on the same road as the Mandala Manager's House but slightly closer to Blantyre and on the left as one heads into Blantyre.

Sanjika Palace, the residence of the Life President, Dr H. Kamuzu Banda, is visible from certain areas at the top of the hill to the immediate west of Blantyre centre and is reached along Independence Drive. It is not open to visitors. Although there are no signs warning the visitor against taking photographs in the immediate vicinity, note that photography is actually prohibited.

For those so inclined, a visit to the Carlsberg Breweries might prove to be interesting. Carlsberg Beer is brewed in Blantyre under Danish supervision and sold as the very popular Carlsberg "Greens" and "Browns" and black stout. The factory, which is situated in Chichiri facing onto Makata Road, welcomes visitors. A guided tour can be arranged by phoning Carlsberg and making an appointment (see page 185 for telephone number).

The tobacco auctioneering floors in Limbe are a hive of activity for approximately six months of the year (April to September), when Malawi's tobacco crop is auctioned to buyers visiting the country from all over the world. The visitor might find it interesting to see how the buyers respond to the lightning-quick patter of the seasoned auctioneer, which is an almost sing-song blur of sound to the uninitiated ear. (Telephone number on page 185.)

A visit to a tea estate can be organised by phoning the relevant estate and making a mutually convenient appointment (see page 185 for telephone numbers). The best time to visit is during the week between the months of October and April/May.

The Kapichira Falls are the most southerly in the series of cataracts that obstruct navigation along 64 km of the Shire River. The falls are a superb spot for a picnic and are less than an hour's drive from Blantyre. They can be reached by taking the Chikwawa road, which runs down the escarpment with its magnificent views and across the Kamuzu

Bridge on the lower Shire, then turning right into Chikwawa and continuing along the road for approximately 23 km. Unfortunately, there is a strong possibility that a hydro-electric scheme is to be built in the vicinity of the falls.

The Mpatamanga Gorge, which lies further north up the Shire River, also serves as a good picnic spot and walking area. It can be reached by following the road from Blantyre past the Chileka airport for a distance of 53 km. The force of the Shire's waters as they thunder through the rocky channels of the river bed is at its most impressive during or just after the rains. You could be forgiven for wondering why the cataracts along this stretch of river and further downstream don't attract canoeists. The simple reason is that the river houses many crocodile and hippo!

Nkhula Falls further upstream are less impressive than the rapids at Mpatamanga Gorge, but still worth visiting. They can be reached by following the same road past Chileka and then taking the turnoff to the right signposted "Walker's Ferry". The distance to the falls from Blantyre is approximately 45 km.

A guide to Blantyre (numbers refer to map on page 13)

1 Chilomoni township
2 Michiru Mountain
3 Sanjika Palace
4 Mount Soche Hotel
5 Ryall's Hotel
6 Seventh Day Adventist Clinic
7 Air Malawi offices
8 Hong Kong Restaurant
9 Main PTC supermarket
10 Curio shops/stalls
11 Immigration department
12 Times Bookshop
13 Hostaria Restaurant
14 Maxim's Restaurant
15 Melting Pot Restaurant
16 Cinemas
17 Post Office
18 Main Kandodo shop
19 British Council
20 Map Surveys Department

21 Old *boma* offices (now treasury offices)
22 Old Town Hall
23 Blantyre Sports Club
24 Blantyre bus depot
25 Grace Bandawe Hostel
26 Blantyre Mission
27 Church of St Michael's and All Angels
28 Nyambadwe Cottage
29 Ndirande Mountain
30 Carlsberg Breweries
31 Blantyre Market
32 Mandala Manager's House
33 Old Mandala Mess
34 Queen Elizabeth Central Hospital
35 Chichiri Industrial Area
36 Greek Church and Hellenic Club
37 Polytechnic
38 Malawi Broadcasting Corporation
39 Police Headquarters (Southern Region)
40 Kamuzu Stadium
41 French Cultural Centre
42 Civic Centre
43 Museum of Malawi
44 Soche Mountain
45 Independence Arch
46 Limbe Tobacco Auction floors
47 Limbe Country Club
48 Gangecraft Curios workshop
49 Macoha Weaving Centre
50 Malawi Railways Lake Service offices
51 Limbe Station
52 Limbe bus depot
53 Shire Highlands Hotel
54 Chisakalime Hotel
55 Limbe Market
56 National Parks and Wildlife Offices, Southern Region

Zomba

Zomba cannot be classed as a city although it is a major town with a large part to play in Malawi's history as its former administrative capital. It nestles at the foot of the magnificent Zomba Plateau (2 085 m at its summit), a visit to which should be a mandatory item on any itinerary.

At one time during the colonial era, this charming town was known as "the most beautiful capital in the Commonwealth". Today, the transformation of Zomba into a university town has ensured that its peaceful character is maintained.

Zomba also houses the parliamentary buildings, where members of Parliament meet for their annual deliberations. Its open-air market has a good reputation for offering the best vegetables in Malawi. The two major supermarket chains, PTC and Kandodo, are both represented and there are a fair number of small shops in the Asian quarter.

Zomba first came into being when it was selected as a potentially viable mission site because of its plentiful water supply from the Mulunguzi stream, with its source on the plateau. The fact that it was set in beautiful surroundings and boasted a temperate climate set the seal on its choice as the seat of the colonial administration.

The missionary John Buchanan, who set about building a sugar mill and small house on the Mulunguzi stream, persuaded the British consul Hawes to provide military support for the small settlement. Permission was granted in 1886.

Further factors in Zomba's favour were that it was considered a more suitable place than Blantyre from which to monitor the slave-trade traffic that passed from the south of Mulanje and along the plains to the east of Zomba on its journey to the lake and ultimately to the slave-markets of Zanzibar. In addition, it was thought to be far enough away from the squabbles between the Blantyre settlers over apportionment of land to provide some welcome respite for those administering the territory.

The settlement was established as the administrative capital in 1891 by the first Commissioner of the British protectorate, Sir Harry Johnston, who moved into the Residency (built in 1887) situated across the road from the Parliament buildings. Now known as the Government Hostel, it houses some of the representatives of the National Assembly when Parliament is sitting. It also serves as a resthouse for members of the public. The Residency's gardens were originally terraced and designed by Alexander Whyte of Edinburgh's Royal Botanical Gardens.

Across the road from the Government Hostel are the Secretariat and Parliament buildings, built on the site of the original building, which was destroyed by fire in 1919.

State House, whose walls are visible from the road leading up to the plateau, was originally the home of Sir Alfred Sharpe, who became

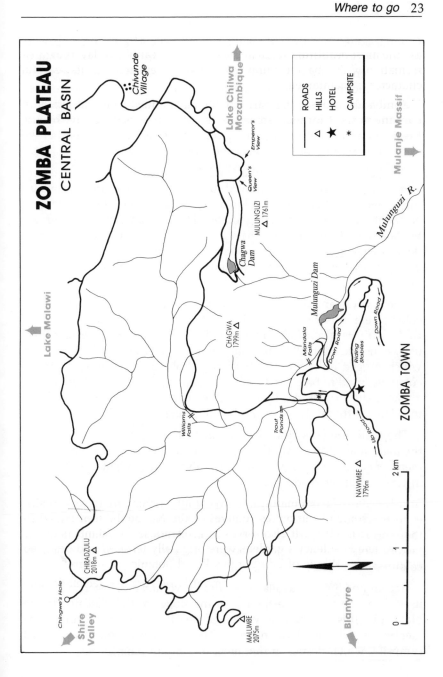

ZOMBA PLATEAU
CENTRAL BASIN

Chivunde Village

Lake Chilwa
Mozambique

Mulanje Massif

Emperor's View

Queen's View

MULUNGUZI △ 1761m

Chagwa Dam

Mulunguzi R.

CHAGWA △ 1799m

Mulunguzi Dam

Mandala Falls

Down Road

Down Road

Riding Stables

Lake Malawi

ROADS
HILLS △
HOTEL ★
CAMPSITE *

ZOMBA TOWN

Williams Falls

Trout Ponds

Up Road

NAWIMBE △ 1796m

CHIRADZULU △ 2018m

Chingwe's Hole

Shire Valley

MALUMBE △ 2075m

Blantyre

N

0   1   2 km

Commissioner and Consul-General of Nyasaland after the departure of Sir Harry Johnston. Sharpe chose the site in preference to that of the Residency, which he believed fell victim to the chill descending from the mountain in the late afternoon. Built originally as a six-roomed bungalow in 1898, its various tenants have added to it and altered it over the years. Nowadays, it serves as one of the residences of the Life President and is not open to the public. Note that photography in the immediate vicinity of the property is not permitted.

Zomba remained the capital until 1975, when many government administration offices were moved to Lilongwe. One of the reasons for this move was that the old colonial buildings which housed the government offices were becoming too small for the expanding government bureaucracy. Conveniently, the vacated government offices and residences were put to good use in accommodating the expanding University of Malawi, whose main campus, Chancellor College, was opened in 1973.

The town's rambling architectural style is largely reminiscent of the colonial era. Visitors may find a visit to the old Zomba Gymkhana Club, with its beautifully situated golf-course, rather interesting. Partially constructed in 1923, the club represented the crux of colonial life, which hinged on sport and socialising. Polo, a favourite sport of the colonials, used to be played on the gymkhana field, which also proved a useful site for parades by the regiments of the King's African Rifles to celebrate the birthday of the British monarch.

The KAR (King's African Rifles) War Memorial, which is visible from the main road at the Blantyre entrance to Zomba, commemorates those members of the King's African Rifles (Nyasaland) regiments who died in service during World War I.

Fishing enthusiasts may enjoy a visit to the fishing fly factory, which exports worldwide. The factory is said to be one of the four largest in the world today in terms of production. Apart from fishing flies, the factory workers also fashion brooches and earrings from magnificently coloured feathers.

Accommodation is available at the Government Hostel in Zomba itself or at the forestry resthouse on the slopes of the plateau. On the plateau itself is the splendidly situated Ku-chawe Inn, the former summer house of the Smithyman family. The plateau also houses a secluded campsite, which nestles in the midst of verdant pine forests.

Zomba is only 69 km from Blantyre, to which it is joined by a tarred road in relatively good condition. The Zomba–Blantyre road used to be the main route from Blantyre to the lake and the Central and Northern Regions before the Blantyre–Mwanza–Balaka road was opened in 1989.

Mzuzu

Mzuzu is the administrative and commercial headquarters of the Northern Region. Founded in 1949, this small "one-horse" town was given city status in 1985, mainly to set the seal on its destiny as the gateway to the less active Northern Region.

It is served by the modern Mzuzu Hotel, resthouses, several stores, service garages, an airport, car hire facilities and a hospital. The Mzuzu Club has a nine-hole golf-course.

Mzuzu itself does not offer the tourist much more than a convenient stopover place from which to visit the surrounding territory. The city lies on the inland plateau just to the north of the magnificent Viphya Plateau with its extensive pine plantations. This superb venue for a picnic is a short drive away from the city.

Heading north from Mzuzu lie the Nyika Plateau and Vwaza Marsh on the M1 via Rumphi and the superbly situated Livingstonia Mission on the Khondowe Plateau overlooking the lake.

Alternatively, the interesting village of Nkhata Bay lies to the south-east on the lakeshore and further south, Chintheche with its fine beach and small hotel can be reached along the M12 in less than two hours.

Ten kilometres further south of Chintheche lies New Bandawe, the mission station which was established in the 1920s by the missionaries of the Church of Central Africa Presbyterian (CCAP). In this area, just a few kilometres south, is Old Bandawe, formerly the mission station established by the missionaries after they abandoned the first Livingstonia mission at Cape Maclear for reasons of ill-health. This same factor put paid to the Old Bandawe mission, which was abandoned after only three years of occupation and re-established at New Livingstonia, further north adjacent to the Nyika Plateau on the escarpment overlooking the lake.

Livingstonia Mission is accessible from Mzuzu via Njakwa Gorge and Mumbwe Plateau (see page 61 for more information about the Livingstonia Mission).

If you are heading for Tanzania, travel through Mzuzu and continue to Karonga on the M1 via Chiweta, where the road joins a scenic lake-shore drive.

THE LAKE AND LAKESHORE

It has to be said that a great deal of what Malawi is, is defined by her lake. And, if one misses a visit to the lake, one has missed a wonderful opportunity of getting to know the true Malawi.

Since about 500 BC the lake has attracted man, who saw it as an ideal place to live, to explore and exploit, or simply to revel in its stunning unspoilt beauty. The lake has been the scene of bloody massacres be-tween tribes long gone, as well as a horrific Arab slave trade which terrorised its inhabitants and also resulted in a large proportion of them converting to the Muslim faith. It was even the scene of the first naval "battle" and British naval victory of World War I (see page 30).

Remaining largely unchanged, Lake Malawi today fulfils a vital eco-nomic function as Malawi's biggest tourist attraction as well as an end-less supplier of fish.

The lake occupies one fifth of the total land mass of Malawi, stretch-ing 575 km in length and 85 km at its widest point. This vast inland sea, part of the Great African Rift Valley, is fed by 14 rivers and drained by only one. The Shire River begins its course to the sea at the lake's southern tip, and, odd as it may seem, accounts for the dispersal of only one per cent of the lake's volume annually.

The third largest lake in Africa, Lake Malawi also ranks twelfth in size in world terms. From 474 m above sea-level, its waters reach depths of 704 m, about 230 m below sea-level, making it the fourth deepest in the world. The deeper sections of this non-tidal lake are found in its northern reaches, where the precipitous sides of the mountains form-ing the walls of the Rift Valley are at their steepest. Oxygen is absent at such depths, making the waters devoid of any form of life, conse-quently fish are more plentiful in the southern portion of the lake.

An important feature of the lake is its abundance of fish, which includes the rare *mbuna* or rock fish, sought after by aquarists all over the world for its unusual behaviour and vivid colouring.

With over 350 endemic (i.e. occurring nowhere else) species of fish swimming in the waters of Lake Malawi National Park and with be-tween 500 and 1 000 species in the entire lake, it is said that Lake

Malawi contains more species than any other lake in the world. The mainstay of its edible harvests, the *chambo* (*Oreochromis* spp.), supplies a large part of the population's protein intake.

The lake supplies employment to many thousands of Malawians who are involved as canoe and net makers and as fishermen and fish traders. A sight that is synonymous with the very essence of Malawi is that of the fisherman in his dugout canoe or *bwato*, a craft made out of a hollowed-out tree trunk and which requires a delicate sense of balance to manoeuvre.

In the villages the visitor will also come across large, wooden racks covered with thousands of tiny silver fish drying in the sun. This is one means of preservation which is used to ensure that the fish reaches the customer in the more distant inland markets in edible condition. Fish are also preserved by wood smoking over a traditional pit fire or modern kiln but although this is a superior method of preservation, it is proving to be problematic as it becomes more and more difficult to obtain wood.

Lake Malawi's tranquil but occasionally unpredictable waters are fringed by golden shores unsullied by pollution, and dotted with lush palm, mango, avocado and banana trees, making it the embodiment of a tropical paradise.

The Malawi government appreciates the importance of tourism and has been careful not to allow a wholesale commercialisation of the lakeshore. Consequently, the tourist who truly wishes to "get away from it all" will certainly value the lake's unspoilt nature. There is no such thing as a crowded beach in Malawi, except in the immediate vicinity of villages. Even when lakeshore resorts are fully occupied, you won't have to fight for your own patch of sand.

Although a visit to the lake can be a rewarding experience all year round, the best times are usually towards the end of the rainy season, in April or May when temperatures are likely to be cooler, and in August and September when it is still not too hot to suntan and the water is warm enough for swimming. (For lake temperature table see page 136.)

June and July might be a little bit too cool for some people although the temperatures are by no means cold, while October, November and December are likely to be the hottest months, making suntanning a risky experience. January, February and March are the height of the rainy season, although the visitor can be rewarded by some very good weather.

In terms of wind, the calmest months at the lake are from March to May. For the larger part of the year, a south-easterly wind prevails but changes to a more northerly direction during the rains. The winds are at their strongest between August and October.

There's more to see in the way of settlements, hotels, campsites and historical sites along the southern edge of the lakeshore than there is further north where the central and, more particularly, the northern lakeshores are still largely untouched by tourism. However, some say that, with its steep embankments forming the walls of the Rift Valley, the northern lakeshore offers scenery far more spectacular than that seen in the south.

In the light of the above, you are better off touring the southern lakeshore by vehicle and, if you have the time, enjoying the northern lakeshore from the decks of the m.v. *Ilala II*, a vessel which plies the waters of Lake Malawi on a week-long round trip. This 620 ton twin-screw vessel carries 10 cabin-class and 350 lower-deck passengers and offers the best vantage point for the viewing of the lake's immensity, its many moods and varied scenery. Leaving every Friday on its six-day round trip from Monkey Bay, the vessel calls at Makanjila, Chipoka, Nkhotakota, Likoma Island, Chizimulu Island, Nkhata Bay, Usisya, Ruarwe, Mlowe, Chitimba, and Chilumba.

Another vessel, the m.v. *Mtendere*, also plies the lake's waters, offering a marine bus service to its dwellers, many of whose homes would be inaccessible by any other means. The *Mtendere* does not offer cabin-class accommodation. However, it does offer the more adventurous tourist the opportunity of travelling side-by-side with Malawians and getting to experience the "real" Malawi, something which the typical package tour is unlikely to offer.

Other lakes

Justifiably overshadowed by their larger sister are three smaller lakes: Lake Malombe, Lake Chilwa and Lake Chiuta. Lake Malombe lies 8 km south of Lake Malawi, to which it is linked by an outlet overflow. It is a shallow stretch of water 29 km long and 14 km wide and conceivably once formed part of Lake Malawi. It is visible to the left of the road that leads from Mangochi to Liwonde.

The outlet linking Lake Malombe to Lake Malawi contains the interesting phenomenon of floating islands. These are clumps of tangled vegetation, mainly reeds, that break off from river mouths after flash floods. The floating mass of rotting vegetation, with roots extending about one metre underwater, probably does not contain actual soil, but rather a type of compact humus.

The larger islands may support fauna such as snakes, frogs, birds and possibly even otters. Given the opportunity of landing on a beach the masses will immediately attempt to root and re-establish themselves. Otherwise they generally get swept southwards towards and into the Shire River, where they may become attached to established reedbeds lining the river.

Lake Chilwa lies further to the south along the eastern border with Mozambique. Although it is a small lake it has abundant fishing stocks and birdlife. The lake is surrounded by swampland and, being completely enclosed, it is subject to a high degree of evaporation.

The smallest of Malawi's lakes is Lake Chiuta, which lies to the north of Lake Chilwa and is split by the Mozambican border.

None of these lakes is easily accessible, nor do they have the type of beaches that would interest the tourist. However, birdlovers are sure to find a wide variety of waterfowl, especially on the eastern shore of Lake Malombe. Should you wish to visit these lakes, only do so in the presence of a local guide and take great care not to wander into Mozambican territory unintentionally.

Mangochi

Located on the west bank of the Shire River, just a few kilometres from the southern tip of the lake, the site was originally known as Fort Johnston. The name was taken from the fort built some 2 km upstream and on the opposite bank in 1891.

Named after Sir Harry Johnston, the country's first Commissioner and Consul General in colonial times, the fort was established as a strategic control point for the surveillance of slave trade traffic. Thousands of slaves would pass through the area, their forced destination being the slave markets of Zanzibar.

The fort's first site was found to be unhealthy and it was moved six years later to its present location some kilometres further south where a settlement was established. In February 1899 the settlement was declared a township and continued to derive its importance from the fact that it was a stronghold for British troops and constituted the headquarters of the Protectorate's naval force. After independence the township was renamed Mangochi.

Situated on the edge of a plain dotted with *Borassus* palm trees, Mangochi houses the offices of the district administration, a post office, police station and hospital as well as several stores and petrol stations which are able to carry out basic repairs to stranded vehicles.

The visitor might notice the spacious layout of the streets, the result of the earliest examples of town-planning in Central Africa. Decorative grass mats, baskets, raffia work and cane chairs which can be viewed and purchased on the sides of the road approaching Mangochi are made by local villagers.

A visit to Malindi Potteries store, unobtrusively tucked away on a clearing off the main road into Mangochi, might prove worth while. Prices are cheap although the selection is rather limited.

If the visitor wishes to see a wider selection, it is possible to visit Malindi Potteries itself, about 19 km from Mangochi. To reach the potteries, cross the river onto the spur of land that juts up the eastern side of the lake. Malindi can be reached by turning left off the main road onto a signposted dirt track, which should be followed for about 10 km. Use of the road is not recommended to drivers of ordinary vehicles during the rainy season and it may still present problems during the dry season.

At the potteries, you can be taken on a guided tour of the factory, which is charmingly situated just a stone's throw away from the lake. The potteries' shop offers a wide variety of attractive items glazed in various shades from deep blue to brown. (See section on pottery, page 91.)

Also consider sparing some time to visit the Lake Malawi Museum, which offers a peep into local natural history and the culture of the lakeshore dwellers. The museum is situated just down the road from the Catholic church, on the premises of the former Lake Nyasa Yacht and Gymkhana Club, which was opened in 1901.

An interesting item to be found in the museum is a model of the bridge belonging to the vessel *Gwendolen*, which earned a place in history when her crew captured a German vessel stationed on the lake during the first naval battle of World War I. As the only British gunboat on the lake during 1914, the H.M.S. *Gwendolen* shared the lake with a German gunboat, the *Hermann von Wissman*, stationed in German-occupied territory on the eastern shore.

Ironically, the *Gwendolen*'s captain, Commander E.L. Rhoades, had prior to the outbreak of war enjoyed an amicable drinking relationship with the German boat's captain. The two were said to have planned mutually enjoyable rendezvous at a number of small lake ports. However, when Rhoades was unexpectedly ordered to "sink, burn or otherwise destroy" the *Hermann von Wissman*, on 8 August 1914, the boat set off in search of the German vessel. The *Von Wissman* was eventually found laid up out of the water and under repair at a small port on the eastern shore of the lake in German East Africa (now Tanzania).

Historical evidence has it that on sighting the vessel, the *Gwendolen's* crew opened fire and eventually scored a hit. This resulted in the alarmed, but casually clad, figure of the German captain jumping into a dinghy and frenziedly rowing out to meet the *Gwendolen*, where in perplexity he demanded an explanation for his friend's behaviour. It transpired that the *Von Wissman's* port had not been in telegraphic contact with the nearest German administration centre and the captain had thus been completely unaware that Germany was in a state of war.

The German ship was then immobilised by Rhoades and his crew and their prisoner of war was taken to captivity at a port on the British lakeshore.

A further reminder of the H.M.S. *Gwendolen* still visible in Mangochi is the vessel's Hotchkiss gun, which stands near the town's clock tower. The clock tower was erected in 1903, as a memorial to Queen Victoria, near the bridge that crosses the Shire River. A plaque set into the clock tower also commemorates those who drowned when the m.v. *Viphya* sank in 1946 just three months after it had been commissioned. A storm in the northern section of the lake caused its worst disaster, claiming 145 victims.

To continue your exploration of the southern lakeshore villages and resorts, turn right at the Mangochi T-junction with the M15 and head north-west in the direction of Monkey Bay. Palm Beach Leisure Resort is signposted off the main road. Just over 1 km towards the lake, the resort lies close to where the mouth of the Shire River joins the lake.

As yet uncompleted, the resort comprises six-bedded self-catering chalets and a tent and caravan camping site. Situated adjacent to a nature sanctuary rich in birdlife, the resort aims to attract the more outdoor-orientated person. There are plans to provide facilities for skiing, windsurfing and sailing.

A few kilometres further along the M15, after taking the signposted turnoff to the right and following a dirt road through a rather picturesque village, you will come to Maldeco Fisheries.

Maldeco is the site of the first commercial fisheries established at Lake Malawi. Depending on the season and general availability, many different types of fresh and frozen fish, including whole *chambo*, are available for sale to the visitor. If you do visit the fisheries, also ask for smoked *kampango* (catfish), which is delicious when eaten cold, and *mpasa*, known as lake salmon. Although it is unrelated to the Atlantic salmon, it does resemble it in taste.

The visitor should be aware that if fish is bought off the street from local fishermen or hawkers, it should be checked for freshness before purchase. If the fish has no smell, is pink under the gills, and the skin springs back leaving no depression when poked with a finger, then it can be considered safe to eat.

It is best not to buy the undersized *chambo*, for apart from the fact that there may not be much flesh on them, it is also an oblique way of discouraging the locals from depleting the future generations of *chambo* before they reach maturity and have a chance to breed.

Some 23 km north of Mangochi lies Nkopola Lodge and Leisure Centre campsite. The hotel's comfortable facilities have recently been extended and upgraded and apart from hotel rooms set back in a small cliff-face, there are a number of modern chalets just a stone's throw from a beautiful beach. Those hotel residents who are accommodated in the aforementioned rooms should not be surprised when they are ogled by voyeuristic monkeys through the skylights in their rooms!

Nkopola Lodge has a shop as well as a petrol service station at its entrance. The shop stocks a number of souvenirs and items that might come in handy such as books, sunglasses and suntan lotion. A large variety of curios of both the wooden and grass variety are also sold by locals at the entrance to the hotel grounds.

Situated a few hundred metres along the beach at Nkopola and also accessible by road (turn right at the signpost as you drive towards the lodge from the main road) is a leisure centre which forms part of the hotel. The leisure centre has its own permanent tented camping site and ablution and catering facilities, although visitors to the centre are able to use the hotel's catering and sporting facilities, the latter being available at reduced prices.

Some 5 km further north along the main road is Club Makokola, a more visually attractive hotel, which doesn't necessarily have better catering and accommodation facilities than Nkopola Lodge, although it does have its own airstrip and swimming pool. The hotel is composed of individual thatched cottages which are dotted about a beautifully maintained lawn that fronts a wide stretch of beach. A specially built kiosk houses some enterprising curio sellers several metres before the entrance to the hotel.

The next lakeshore settlement likely to be of interest to the tourist is the village of Monkey Bay, further north along the main road. Lake settlements between Club Mak and Monkey Bay mostly comprise small fishing villages interspersed with a few cottages privately owned by individuals and companies.

Monkey Bay

Monkey Bay is situated at the end of the M15, a drive that takes the visitor through sleepy plains dotted with baobabs and palm trees. The only wildlife seen on the road are a few baboons and monkeys, and the occasional snake, although you might glimpse a hippo as one was reportedly "run over" and killed on the road fairly recently.

The entrance to this scenic bay is guarded by an island and the bay itself is ringed with hills making its waters exceptionally calm. It is a natural harbour and an ideal docking place for the headquarters of the Malawi Army Naval Unit and the Malawi Railways Lake Service.

The two main passenger vessels operating on the lake, the m.v. *Ilala II* and the m.v. *Mtendere*, are serviced and berthed at Monkey Bay's dockyards and workshops before commencing their round trips to the northern section of the lake and back each week.

Not much else happens at this sleepy bay, where it seems that to-morrow is another day that can take care of itself. However, the visitor may like to visit the Monkey Bay Club, where he could bump into the captains of the vessels and have a game of snooker with them while downing a cold "Green", the locally-brewed Carlsberg beer.

There is also a post office with telephone facilities, a dry-season landing strip, a well-stocked supermarket and a service station where petrol is sold. If your vehicle does happen to break down in the vicinity of Monkey Bay, try contacting the Malawi Railways workshops, whose personnel are likely to be very helpful with minor repairs.

The serious fisherman may be interested to visit the Department of Fisheries, which is situated to the northern end of Monkey Bay at the end of the road that runs past the clubhouse. The Fisheries officer is said to be always happy to offer advice and information regarding Malawi's diverse fish species.

While in the Monkey Bay area, particularly closer to the dockyards, be certain to seek permission before taking photographs.

From Monkey Bay one would be well advised to visit Cape Maclear, arguably one of the most beautiful of all the coves of Lake Malawi.

Cape Maclear

Heading back towards Mangochi from Monkey Bay along the M15, after about 6 km a signposted dirt road leads off to the right of the main road. This 18 km long bumpy road, which is mostly untarred, leads to Cape Maclear, Otter Point, the Golden Sands campsite, Stevens' Resthouse in Chembe village and a number of private cottages.

The approach to Cape Maclear is said by some to be the most beautiful drive in all Malawi. It is quite possible to imagine that you are the only visitors to this garden of Eden, which seems to have been untouched by man for thousands of years. The road winds its way along the bottom of a valley lined with steep rocky hills that undoubtedly shelter the secretive leopard. Monkeys and baboons are often seen on the road, or scampering up large boulders that may be covered with searching roots of trees.

In 1861, while exploring the area, Livingstone named the cape after his friend Sir Thomas Maclear, then Astronomer Royal at Cape Town. The headquarters of the first Livingstonia Mission of the Free Church of Scotland were established here in 1875 as a memorial to the famous missionary-explorer. The site was chosen for its sheltered bay, which protected the missionary boats from storms buffeting the neighbouring shoreline.

However, the Scottish missionaries who so industriously set about establishing a mission station were beset by a number of obstacles, the most damaging of which was the death of five missionaries as a result of illness. In an attempt to establish an alternative, healthier site, they moved the mission much further north to Bandawe in 1881 (just south of present-day Chintheche on the western shore of the lake), before abandoning that site two years later and finally establishing the present-day Livingstonia Mission near the Nyika Plateau even further north.

Despite Cape Maclear's unsuitability as a mission site, it continued to be used as a fuelling station from which the various lake steamers were supplied with wood. By 1941 its value as a potential site for a luxury hotel began to be appreciated, and after a number of setbacks, a hotel finally opened its doors in 1948.

Towards the end of 1949 BOAC (now British Airways) launched a regular flying boat service whose Short Solent flying boats landed at Cape Maclear *en route* from Southampton docks in England to the Vaal Dam near Johannesburg in South Africa. The *Solent*, a four-engined craft carrying 28 passengers and a crew of 8, proved to be a comfortable – but slow – form of travel. Only one year after the service began, it was withdrawn in favour of faster planes which reduced flying times between South Africa and the United Kingdom.

The road leading to Cape Maclear proved to be rather heavy going, particularly during the wet season. This made it difficult for visitors to reach the hotel by car, leaving boats and planes as the only other means of access. Consequently, after the flying boat service was withdrawn, tourism to Cape Maclear dwindled to such an extent that the decision was taken in 1951 to close the hotel and ship whatever structures could be moved to a new hotel site at Senga Bay near Salima, an area more accessible to tourists. Since then there have been a number of plans to redevelop the site and build a hotel to international standards, but to date no marked progress has been made on the project.

The site of the old mission, the missionaries' graves nearby and Otter Point, which forms the western end of the bay, are all protected under the Monuments Act and are encompassed within an 87 km^2 area known as Lake Malawi National Park.

The park includes an area of water lying within a 100 m boundary of the shore (see section on National Parks, page 48). A trail leads from the right of the grave site up Nkhunguni, which at 1 143 m is the tallest hill in the park and offers superb views to climbers and hikers.

At Cape Maclear itself, within the Lake Malawi National Park, lies a decrepit resort known as Golden Sands. There have been plans to demolish it for ages but if it still stands one can take advantage of very basic accommodation in its rondavels or use its camping site.

Alternatively one can try further north (1 or 2 km as the crow flies) along the coastline for accommodation at Stevens' Resthouse, which is just inside the local fishing village of Chembe, renowned for its *Gule Wamkulu* tribal dancers.

The resthouse is situated on the beach overlooking a bay ringed by Thumbi Island West and Domwe Island. For a reasonable fee local fishermen hire out their dugouts and small fishing boats for trips to the islands. Mr Stevens serves basic but tasty food and cold "Greens", which is just about all one needs on a gloriously hot and sunny day at the lake.

Salima

Salima is a town lying some 22 km inland from the nearest resort – Livingstonia Beach Hotel – at Senga Bay. Twenty-seven kilometres south of Salima is Chipoka, a major lakeshore port linked with Malawi's main centres by rail and road services. Salima is also connected with Lilongwe by a 106 km single-strip tar road.

The settlement consists of a tranquil village surrounded by mango, pawpaw, banana and cotton plantations. It has the same air about it that is found in so many other Malawian villages, giving the impression that the rest of the world might be at war but things will carry on here at the same steady pace they have done for centuries. Fortunately for the tourist who seeks respite from the rat race, this relaxed attitude can be quite contagious.

The town comprises government offices, stores and oil installation, with a dry-season airstrip that services small aircraft. It also has a number of very basic resthouses and nightclubs and its local open-air market is a fair source of fruit and vegetables.

Tragically, during 1989, Salima was hit by an earthquake as well as floods which left a large number of its inhabitants, who were completely unprepared for such a disaster, homeless. At the height of the floods, villagers were seen travelling about their daily tasks in dugouts, while others were fishing on the side of the road.

In this area in particular the tourist might come across the strangely dressed *Gule Wamkulu* tribal dancers parading on the road. The principal dancers are dressed in skins and have strips of rags and feathers tied together in a headdress covering their faces. Often one of their members can be seen walking on very tall stilts with many cheering attendants in tow. The visitor may wish to take photographs of the procession but should be wary of paying too much by way of a gratuity in return for this favour. It's best not to get too involved in such a procession but rather keep a safe distance. Note that young children might get frightened by the sight of the strangely dressed figures.

Between Salima and the lake lies a marshy area which is noted for its rich birdlife. The aquarist will also find a visit to the Tropical Fish Aquarium just off the M5 rather interesting. It is to this centre that *mbuna*, the small but vividly coloured rock fish, are brought from all parts of the lake before being shipped out of the country to tropical fish enthusiasts all over the world.

Livingstonia Beach

It is only recently that this area has come to be known as Livingstonia Beach. Although the name of the locality, Senga Bay, has remained the same, the beach was formerly known as Grand Beach and was the site of the old Grand Beach Hotel, now considerably refurbished and known as the Livingstonia Beach Hotel. The hotel comprises rooms and rondavels and is situated just off a pleasant beach. Facilities include a fairly sophisticated menu, a large swimming pool and the use of a wide range of watersport equipment for windsurfing, parasailing, sailing and skiing. The hotel also arranges guided tours of the surrounding area. Adjacent to the hotel is a campsite with ablution blocks.

Apart from the watersports, the visitor may enjoy a ride in a dugout canoe to the nearby island, about 2 km offshore. Villagers are usually fairly keen to take tourists out for a small fee. However, the ride is not recommended for those who are likely to feel unsafe in these very unstable craft despite the fact that the boatmen are extremely skilled at manoeuvring the dugouts.

On the other side of Namikombe Point, just to the north of the hotel and facing onto Leopard Bay, is an interesting fishing village, the closest point to the eastern shore of the lake. From this point, since time immemorial, Arab dhows have conducted crossings, ferrying both cargo and passengers from one side of the lake to the other. The village can easily be reached in less than half an hour by footpath from the hotel.

For those interested in walking, there are paths leading to the top of Senga Hill and the adjacent Nankhumba Hill, which offer fine views over the lake. Just on the northern side of Senga Hill are some swamps, which form the home base for a herd of hippo. It is possible to drive there from the hotel in about fifteen minutes.

It's worthwhile remembering that hippo are not playful harmless creatures as depicted in children's books and TV programmes. They are unpredictable, deadly animals which are found all around the lakeshore. Their most active period is at night when temperatures are coolest and when they can emerge from their watery habitat to graze without risk of being sunburnt. Hence the warning by most lakeshore hotels to evening strollers to stay off the beach and near the hotel after dark and before sunrise. Swimmers should not venture into the water during the hours of darkness.

During the day hippo tend to stay in the water, in which they can be submerged for five to six minutes at a time, making their presence very difficult to detect. If you are unsure of the presence of hippo, your best bet is to ask a local if there are any about.

In the light of the above, if you choose to walk in the swampland you also take a risk as hippos are especially dangerous when returning to their aquatic territory after grazing, since they dislike finding anything between themselves and their homeground. Although the hippo seems large and cumbersome, it can reach speeds of up to 30 km/h and a human being probably would not be able to outrun an enraged hippo.

Nkhotakota

Reputed to be the largest traditional village in Central and Southern Africa, Nkhotakota is also distinguished by the fact that it was the largest Arab slave-trading depot on the lake. By 1870, at the height of the slave-trading activities, approximately 10 000 slaves are said to have passed through the town each year.

David Livingstone attempted to land here in 1861 but was prevented from doing so by the heavy surf. He returned overland from the south two years later and while in the area tried to persuade the reigning chief, who represented the Sultan of Zanzibar in administering the slave trade, to abandon his activities.

The town still bears the mark of Arab influence as many of its inhabitants follow the Muslim faith and some can still be seen wearing Arab-style skullcap and characteristic, voluminous tunic.

In more modern times, His Excellency, the Life President, Dr H. Kamuzu Banda, made his mark on the town when he held his first major political rally here after being released from prison in Gwelo, Rhodesia in 1960. The event was marked by the naming of a central square as Freedom Square.

The town offers accommodation in a number of basic resthouses. There is also a post office, hospital and a few grocery shops. The *Ilala* and *Mtendere* call at Nkhotakota, anchoring offshore on their way in both northerly and southerly directions.

A 105 km tarred road (S33) links Nkhotakota with the Lilongwe–Salima road in the south while the 58 km S53 is the link with the next settlement of Dwanga in the north.

The Nkhotakota Game Reserve (see section on Game reserves, page 57) lies to the east of the town and can be reached via the M10, an untarred short-cut to Lilongwe.

Dwangwa

Lying about 58 km to the north of Nkhotakota, Dwangwa's main *raison d'être* is its large sugar-cane plantation and processing plant as well as an ethanol production plant, both of which are administered by the Sugar Corporation of Malawi (Sucoma). The factory is also the site of a fledgeling crocodile and prawn farming endeavour.

The plantation, which first came into production in 1979, has a private clubhouse with a well-cared-for nine-hole golfcourse, squash courts, tennis courts and swimming pool. Adjacent to the clubhouse are a number of comfortable self-catering chalets intended for use by the guests and employees of the estate, but which are open to the public by special arrangement (see section on accommodation facilities, page 159).

Chintheche

Continuing north along the untarred S53 lakeshore road for 91 km, the next point of interest to the visitor is Chintheche, which has a small hotel and a fine beach. Chintheche has been earmarked as an important site for the development of the ambitious Viphya Pulp and Paper Project. The town is an ancient canoe-crossing point to the eastern shore of the lake and was, at one point in history, the battlefield between the Tonga tribe and Ngoni invaders.

Ten kilometres south of Chintheche is the so-called New Bandawe, where a mission station was established during the 1920s by missionaries of the Church of Central Africa Presbyterian (CCAP). Some kilometres further south of New Bandawe is the Livingstonia Mission's second site, established after Cape Maclear was abandoned for reasons of ill-health.

The pioneer missionaries were forced to abandon Old Bandawe site for the same reason after only three years, in 1884, after which the third and final site of the mission was established at present-day Livingstonia on the Nyika Plateau overlooking the lake.

Nkhata Bay

Nkhata Bay, some 60 km further north along the winding, untarred S53, which is flanked by the plantations of the Vizara Rubber Estate, is the last town along this stretch of shoreline that is accessible by the road before it veers off away from the lakeshore and into the highlands of Mzuzu.

Nkhata Bay marks the most northerly point reached by David Livingstone, who assumed that the end of the lake was just slightly north of the region. Believing that he had completed his exploration of the lake, he turned off into the hills above Nkhata Bay where he became lost and nearly died.

The town's place in history was anchored by the anti-federation uprising on 3 March 1959, when a blanket state of emergency was declared over Nyasaland. The victims of the uprising are remembered each year on Martyr's Day (3 March), which is a public day of mourning.

This pretty town, said by some to rival Cape Maclear in beauty, is a hive of peaceful activity today and still acts as a major port for the *Ilala* and *Mtendere*, which lie in dock overnight. Chikale Beach, which is worth visiting, lies 3 km further south of Nkhata Bay and can be reached on foot after a 20 minute walk, or by car, depending on the time of year and the state of the road leading to it.

Nkhata Bay is a convenient terminal point for those wishing to combine road travel with a few days aboard the *Ilala*. It is possible to board the *Ilala* further south and sail up to Nkhata Bay before alighting and, having organised for a hire car to meet you on time, to continue your exploration of the north by car before returning to Lilongwe. Alternatively, you could do the trip in reverse, driving to Nkhata Bay after having explored the north by car, and boarding the *Ilala* to sail south to Chipoka or Monkey Bay.

For those wishing to spend a night in Nkhata Bay, accommodation is available at the resthouse next to the old colonial *boma* on the hill.

Chilumba

The small town of Chilumba acts as the terminus for the *Ilala* on its northward journey up the lake. It is possible to stay here, but the resthouse accommodation is very basic.

Karonga

Karonga is the largest town in the most northern section of the lakeshore and is reached by the tarred M1 from Mzuzu. Karonga's place in history was secured by the fact that it was the site of the only military encounter of World War 1 to be fought on Malawian territory between British and German troops in 1914.

A reminder of the military activity that took place in the region is the enormous hollow baobab tree that at one point was fortified and used as an ammunition store. The tree can be seen near the old administrative section of the town.

Accommodation is available at the Karonga Resthouse near the *boma*.

NATIONAL PARKS

The Malawi government is very conscious of its precious wildlife heritage and the need for its conservation. Much is done by the government and the very active Malawi Wildlife Society to stimulate the support of Malawians in preserving wildlife as a national asset. To this end, Malawi has gained a reputation for having developed one of the better wildlife management schemes in Africa. Poachers, usually from neighbouring countries, are hunted down with a vengeance and there is a strict emphasis on controls such as permits and licences necessary for the sale and purchase of ivory.

Despite the government's awareness that the national parks are valuable tourist attractions, they have not been turned into glorified zoos. The existence of the wildlife within them has not been compromised by the building of tarred roads and the provision of large accommodation facilities. In summary, the essence of Africa in all her splendour has been faithfully retained.

There are five national parks in existence today: Nyika, Kasungu, Lake Malawi, Liwonde and Lengwe. The national parks have been developed with the car-bound tourist in mind while the reserves (see page 56) are likely to appeal to those who would prefer to rough it in the bush, in most cases without the benefit of roads or tracks. Hunting is prohibited and when driving in the parks, visitors should adhere to a maximum speed limit of 40 km/h. All types of fire are forbidden outside the game camps and visitors are asked to take great care with the disposal of cigarettes and matches. Firearms and dogs or other pets are not allowed into the parks.

Nyika National Park

Set in one of the most beautiful regions of Malawi and entirely different in character from the rest of tropical Malawi, the Nyika National Park includes most of the high-lying Nyika Plateau in the country's Northern Region.

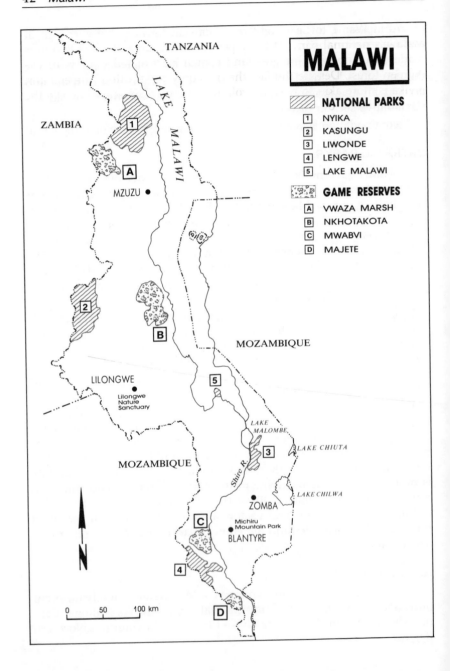

Encompassing an area of over 3 000 km², Nyika is the largest of Malawi's national parks. Ninety per cent of its area above 1 800 m is made up of open, short grassland containing isolated pockets of evergreen forest. Despite the fact that it is only 10° south of the equator, Nyika is more akin to a gently rolling European landscape than to the startling drama of Africa.

Owing to its higher altitude, the climate is much cooler than that encountered in the remainder of Malawi, something which provides a welcome contrast to the sometimes sweltering heat and mosquitoes found at lower altitudes. Gentle summer temperatures that rarely exceed 21,5°C give way to more bracing and invigorating weather in June, July and August, when there is frost about and the Nyika log fires are a welcome distraction.

People with heart conditions should take note that they may be affected by the high altitude (1 800 up to 2 500 m).

The undulating grasslands with deep valleys and streams that run throughout the year provide excellent game-viewing opportunities and superb picnic spots. These are features that the angler can combine with a spot of trout-fishing (see trout-fishing section, page 85) in the park's three dams.

Nyika's long, gracious, sweeping hills stretch as far as the eye can see and house the largest concentration of leopard to be found in the country. The most common animals seen by visitors are reedbuck, zebra, roan and eland, while bushbuck and warthog are often seen and the klipspringer inhabits the rockier areas. Among other animals to be seen are the red duiker, blue duiker, hartebeest and blue monkey.

Nocturnal animals present in the park are the hyena, jackal, serval and civet cats, porcupine, honeybadger and aardvark. The best time to seek out leopard is around sunset or sunrise. Game-viewing overall is most rewarding during the months of November to May inclusive, though at the height of the wet season (February/March) it would be advisable to consider using four-wheel-drive transport.

Several species of high altitude birds have been observed at Nyika. These include Denham's bustard and the red-winged francolin in the grasslands, while the evergreen forest features the cinnamon dove, bar-tailed trogon and starred robin high in the forest canopy. (See For birdwatchers, page 76.) Bird-watching is at its most rewarding during the months of October to December, when many migrant species are present.

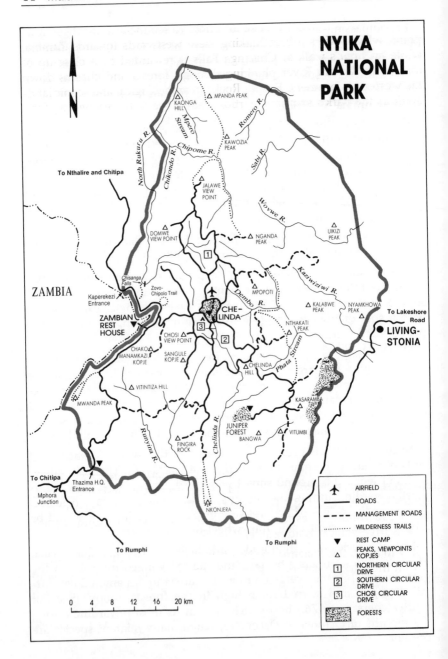

NYIKA NATIONAL PARK

To Nthalire and Chitipa

ZAMBIA

Chisanga Falls

Kaperekezi Entrance

Zovo-Chipolo Trail

ZAMBIAN REST HOUSE

KAONGA HILL

Mpera Stream

Chikondo R.

North Rukuru R.

Chipome R.

MPANDA PEAK

Romero R.

KAWOZIA PEAK

Sabi R.

JALAWE VIEW POINT

Wovwe R.

DOMWE VIEW POINT

NGANDA PEAK

UIKIZI PEAK

Kaziwiziwi R.

MPOPOTI

Dembo R.

CHE-LINDA

KALABWE PEAK

NYAMKHOWA PEAK

To Lakeshore Road

LIVING-STONIA

NTHAKATI PEAK

CHOSI VIEW POINT

CHAKO MANAMKAZI KOPJE

SANGULE KOPJE

Phata Stream

CHELINDA HILL

VITINTIZA HILL

MWANDA PEAK

Runyina R.

Chelinda R.

KASARAMBA

JUNIPER FOREST

BANGWA

VITUMBI

FINGIRA ROCK

To Chitipa

Thazima H.Q. Entrance

Mphora Junction

NKONJERA

To Rumphi

To Rumphi

✈	AIRFIELD
——	ROADS
- - -	MANAGEMENT ROADS
·······	WILDERNESS TRAILS
▼	REST CAMP
△	PEAKS, VIEWPOINTS KOPJES
1	NORTHERN CIRCULAR DRIVE
2	SOUTHERN CIRCULAR DRIVE
3	CHOSI CIRCULAR DRIVE
	FORESTS

0 4 8 12 16 20 km

Places that one should make an effort to see include Domwe view-point, which offers a breathtaking view westwards towards Zambia, while an hour's walk to Chisanga Falls is rewarded by a close-up of the North Rukuru River plunging through forests and chasms down the western escarpment. Fingira Rock, an archeological and scenic land-mark in the park's southern portion, may have to be reached on foot, depending on the condition of the track.

The most southerly viable juniper forest in Africa occurs in the park and a trail and cabin have been established in the forest to give the visitor the best opportunity to appreciate this unusual area (see map).

The display of wildflowers which abound in the grasslands, including proteas, heathers and rare orchids, is at its most spectacular during the rains (December to March). After the ritual burning of the grass to clear the accumulation of combustible material and prevent more destructive fires at the end of the dry season, visitors to the park are treated to a brilliant array of heathers between August and November.

A variety of wilderness trails has been established and visitors are free to walk through to the more remote areas of the park. Walkers should be reasonably fit as trails range from one to five days in duration and involve camping out in tents. Groups are escorted by a trained game scout and porters may be hired if desired. If available for use at the time, park transport can be hired to the start or from the end of the trails, or visitor's vehicles can be driven by a park driver if necessary. All camping and other equipment must be provided by the visitor. (For accommodation details see page 149.)

Access

Access to the park is through the gate at Thazima, which is 67 km from Rumphi, 129 km from Mzuzu and 56 km from Chelinda Camp (see routes section, page 113). The road from Rumphi is untarred and may be in bad condition, especially during the rains when use of a four-wheel-drive vehicle is advisable.

Try to reach the Thazima gate by 16h00 as it is not advisable to drive within the park as darkness descends. A new road to Chelinda Camp has been built from Thazima and its use is recommended as it is more scenic than the old road.

The park has a dry-season airstrip which can be used by charter aircraft.

Kasungu National Park

Covering over 2 000 km², Kasungu National Park lies some 55 km west of the town of Kasungu in the Central Region. The park, which lies at an altitude of just over 1 000 m above sea-level, forms the catchment area for several rivers including the Dwanga, Lingadzi and Lifupa. The park's terrain consists of gently undulating *Brachystegia* woodland which extends westwards to the Zambian border.

The fact that Kasungu National Park is the most accessible to visitors from Malawi's main centres, as well as being home to a wide variety of animal species, has led to Kasungu becoming the most popular of the national parks.

Many species of antelope are to be seen in the park, including bushbuck, hartebeest, impala, duiker and the magnificent kudu and sable. There are also numerous elephant, buffalo, zebra and lion, while leopard and cheetah can be observed on occasion. Species which are occasionally sighted include the hyena, wild dog, serval, bushpig, grysbok, klipspringer and sidestriped jackal. The dam in front of Lifupa Lodge, the visitor's camp, houses some hippo, and baboon and grey monkey are found in some sections of the park.

The best vantage points for game viewing in Kasungu are the watering and grazing areas lying in the valleys of the park's rivers, while birdwatchers will find the small dam at Lifupa Lodge most rewarding.

Despite their size, elephants can become inconspicuous in the dense bush and slow travelling is recommended if they are to be spotted. It is quite possible to unexpectedly find yourself very near or even in the midst of a herd of elephant and if this is the case, make every attempt not to provoke the herd as there is always the risk of an angry elephant charging a car. Never race your engine, as the elephant could construe this as a form of aggression. Nor should you drive towards the herd. Rather reverse as slowly as possible or if this is not feasible, keep your car stationary. In time the herd should move away.

The best time to visit the park for game-viewing purposes is towards the end of the dry season (August–November) when the thicket is least dense and in some parts has been systematically burnt. At this time of year, the water supply begins to dwindle and animals are forced to congregate around the relatively few water-holes remaining in their search for water and food. The best times of day for game viewing are in the early morning and early evening when it is cooler and the animals are more energetic.

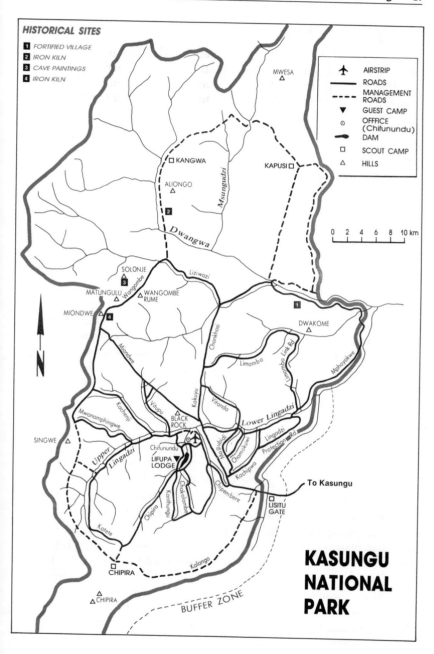

HISTORICAL SITES
1 FORTIFIED VILLAGE
2 IRON KILN
3 CAVE PAINTINGS
4 IRON KILN

✈ AIRSTRIP
— ROADS
--- MANAGEMENT ROADS
▼ GUEST CAMP
⊙ OFFFICE (Chifunundu)
▬ DAM
□ SCOUT CAMP
△ HILLS

0 2 4 6 8 10 km

MWESA △

□ KANGWA

Msungudzi

KAPUSI □

ALIONGO △

2

Dwangwa

SOLONJE △
3
MATUNGULU △

Wangombe

Liziwazi

1

MIONDWE △
4

WANGOMBE RUME △

DWAKOME △

Miondwe

Chankhosi

Limomba

Limomba Link Rd.

Mphayakwe

Mwanamphingwe

Kochenji

Vitupu

Kakyu

Virando

Lower Lingadzi

BLACK ROCK

Lingadzi

SINGWE △

Upper Lingadzi

Chifunundu
LIFUPA LODGE ▼

Kongubidi

Chomchuwe

Kachipwa

Lingadzi Protection Rd.

To Kasungu

Chipra

Konthungu

Chakolombe

Chipembere

LISITU GATE □

Kotere

Kalango

□ CHIPIRA

△ CHIPIRA

BUFFER ZONE

KASUNGU NATIONAL PARK

N

The park has a good network of untarred roads giving the visitor wide access to many different areas. The roads are in a better condition during the dry season, having been graded after the previous season's rains and compacted by traffic.

Some of the park's roads may be closed during the rainy season, depending on the severity of the rainfall. Although unsafe roads are usually marked, the visitor should check with the Department of National Parks and Wildlife on the condition of the roads during the rains and whether use of a four-wheel-drive vehicle is advisable. During March, there is usually only limited access to the Park, which is likely to suit those visitors who merely wish to have a peaceful holiday in beautiful surroundings and not necessarily to seek out game. (For accommodation details see page 149.)

Access

The park entrance is reached by 38 km of mostly untarred road (D187) from the turnoff to Kasungu. The town lies on the main Lilongwe–Mzuzu road and offers the tourist accommodation at the Kasungu Inn. Kasungu is 127 km from Lilongwe, while Lifupa Lodge is 14 km inside the park from the entrance. There is a dry-season grass airstrip at the administration camp, which is about 4 km from the lodge. Petrol is sold at the lodge, subject to availability, while diesel may be available at the administration camp. To be on the safe side rather fill your tank at Kasungu, before entering the park.

Lake Malawi National Park

The world's first freshwater national park is a haven to what is reasonably estimated to be more freshwater fish species than are found in all the waters of both Europe and North America.

Although the park, which is largely focused on Cape Maclear in the southern portion of Lake Malawi, houses land-based fauna and flora, the main reason for its existence is the protection of the vividly coloured *mbuna* or rock fish, which have attracted the keen attention of aquarists worldwide.

Without exception, the *mbuna* are small in size, the largest being no longer than 15 cm. They are largely found in rocky areas where they display the characteristic of never venturing away from their chosen type of habitat. These seemingly invisible boundaries have the effect

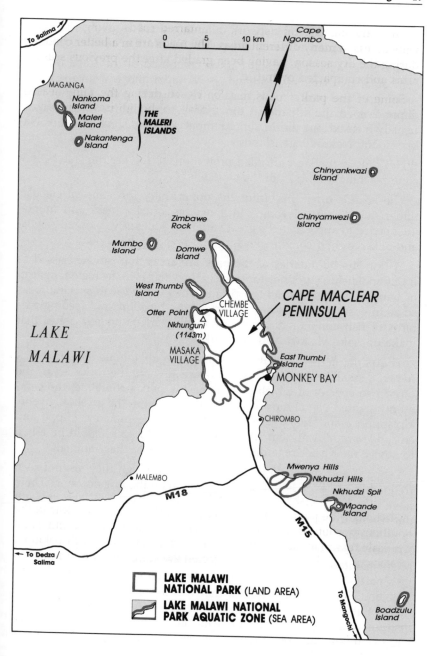

LAKE
MALAWI

THE
MALERI
ISLANDS

Nankoma
Island

Maleri
Island

Nakantenga
Island

MAGANGA

To Salima

Cape
Ngombo

Chinyankwazi
Island

Chinyamwezi
Island

Zimbawe
Rock

Mumbo
Island

Domwe
Island

West Thumbi
Island

Otter Point

CHEMBE
VILLAGE

CAPE MACLEAR
PENINSULA

Nkhunguni
(1143m)

MASAKA
VILLAGE

East Thumbi
Island

MONKEY BAY

CHIROMBO

Mwenya Hills

Nkhudzi Hills

Nkhudzi Spit

MALEMBO

M18

Mpande
Island

To Dedza /
Salima

To Mangochi

M15

Boadzulu
Island

0   5   10 km

☐ **LAKE MALAWI
NATIONAL PARK** (LAND AREA)

▨ **LAKE MALAWI NATIONAL
PARK AQUATIC ZONE** (SEA AREA)

of isolating the different species, allowing them to evolve breeding, feeding and territorial habits independently of other species.

The Lake Malawi National Park is composed of the Cape Maclear Peninsula, two smaller headlands – Nkhudzi and Mwenya – to the south-east, and twelve islands, Domwe, Thumbi West, Thumbi East, Mumbo, Boadzulu, Mpande, Chinyankwazi and Chinyamwezi islands, Zimbawe Rock and the Maleri Archipelago, consisting of Nankoma, Maleri and Nakantenga islands.

Not only is the land afforded protection; so too are the waters, in a zone reaching 100 m from the shoreline.

The islands offer the visitor the opportunity for some spectacular underwater "game viewing". In many cases just a mask and snorkel are needed to appreciate the great variety of brilliantly coloured *mbuna*, and observe their complex feeding and breeding behaviour.

Within the boundaries of the park are areas that can be classed as traditional fishing grounds for some of the villages in the region. Instead of banning fishing outright, legislation has limited it to specific areas so as to ensure minimal disturbance of the breeding and feeding patterns of fish communities endemic to the various aquatic zones that make up Lake Malawi National Park.

The park's terrestrial animals include the ubiquitous dassie or rock hyrax, a small rabbit-like creature which favours the rocky areas; the otter, two species of which exist along the park's shoreline; the commonly sighted vervet monkey and yellow baboon, the grysbok, hyena, klipspringer and zebra as well as the rare blue monkey. Hippo and crocodile are also present within the park and locals should be asked to advise the visitor regarding recent sightings of these animals.

Leopard and serval do inhabit the park although they are not seen frequently and even lion have been sighted on the rare occasion. There have also been reports of elephant drinking from the lake at night during the dry season, although they are not resident in the park. In fact, Mumbo Island was also known in the past as Elephant Island. Although it is approximately 9 km from Cape Maclear, traces of elephant habitation were found there in 1876 when it was investigated by a party of curious missionaries from the Cape Maclear Livingstonia Mission. The lone bull elephant that was indeed found on the island had previously been wounded, a factor, it was thought, that had been instrumental in causing him to swim out to the island. The elephant was eventually killed by the missionaries.

The park is home to a large number of different bird species, the most prominent of which are the breeding colonies of white-breasted cormorants found on Boadzulu and Mumbo islands together with the pied kingfisher and majestic fish eagle, whose piercing and mournful cry often punctuates the tranquillity.

The keen birdwatcher will enjoy a visit to the park's reedbeds and swamps, which support jacana, ibis, egret and a number of species of weaver birds that can be observed nesting from October to June.

A company known as Rift Lake Charters based near to Club Makokola, further south along the shoreline from Cape Maclear, offers the visitor a number of sailing and scuba safaris. These are designed to combine the pleasure of sailing with memorable underwater exploration of the park's shoreline, an experience that has been likened to swimming in a giant aquarium. Alternatively, local fishermen will be only too pleased to accept a small fee for ferrying tourists in dugout canoes to one of the nearby islands.

Those of a historical bent might like to take note of the fact that the first site of the Livingstonia Mission was in the immediate vicinity of the present-day Golden Sands Holiday Camp, which is situated at Cape Maclear (see notes on Cape Maclear, page 34). (For accommodation details see page 169.)

Access

The park can be reached by vehicle along the M15 (Monkey Bay–Mangochi Road) from which the mostly untarred S39 branches off just 6 km south of Monkey Bay. The S39 runs through magnificent scenery for 18 km to Cape Maclear and is negotiable for most of the year (see route section, page 118).

The road passes Mwalamphini, the rock of tribal markings, the path to which is clearly signposted. The rock's face is covered with striations resembling the traditional markings that certain tribes used to carve on their faces. However, the markings have been created by natural geological and weathering forces. Mwalamphini has been declared a national monument.

Cape Maclear is 232 km from Lilongwe, 186 km from Zomba and 265 km from Blantyre.

Liwonde National Park

One of the main attractions of this park, which is situated on the Upper Shire Plain in the Southern Region, is the strongly flowing Shire River. Forming the park's western border, the river is the only outlet for the waters of Lake Malawi, which drain into the Indian Ocean via the Zambezi River. A section of Lake Malombe, between the Shire River and Lake Malawi is incorporated in the northern area of the park.

The lake and river have resulted in the creation of many different types of vegetation, including floodplain, woodland, thicket and swamp. The protection of this vegetation was an important factor in the creation of the 548 km^2 Liwonde National Park in 1973.

Since that time, the more commonly seen inhabitants of the park – hippo, crocodile, elephant, sable and waterbuck – have found an important sanctuary alongside warthog, bushbuck, impala and reedbuck. Leopard and a few lions are regularly seen in the park and its rich and varied birdlife includes the only Malawi population of Lillian's lovebird.

Liwonde's elephant population has a reputation for being one of the most vicious on the subcontinent. This has been attributed to inefficient poaching activities which naturally enrage the wounded animals. A relatively recent report of a visitor's death in the park caused by elephant concerned a priest who left his car to take a photograph. He was apparently trampled to death just a short distance away from his vehicle.

The only viable road in the park leads to Mvuu (hippo) Camp, which is set in charming surroundings on the riverbank (see accommodation, page 152). During the wet season (December to April), depending on the severity of the rainfall, the road may become impassable, in which case the park will be closed to the public. Visitors are advised to make enquiries in advance.

The second half of the dry season (August to November) is the best time for game viewing as this is the time when the animals are likely to be concentrated near the river. Visitors to the park should note that high temperatures are likely to be experienced especially just before the rains.

It is possible to walk in the park if accompanied by a scout. However, although the scout may be armed, the element of risk of attack by a wild animal is still sizeable. Two places of interest to the walker are the Kalunga and Chisuse water-holes, which are used by elephant, sable, kudu, warthog and a variety of birds mainly in the early morning and late afternoon during the dry season. Walkers can also visit Chiunguni Hill, a volcanic cone open on one side, which at 921 m is the highest point of the park. From its summit the hill offers impressive views of the Shire Valley and River.

Visitors may also enter the park by boat throughout the year and travel up the Shire River to Lake Malombe while viewing wildlife. The

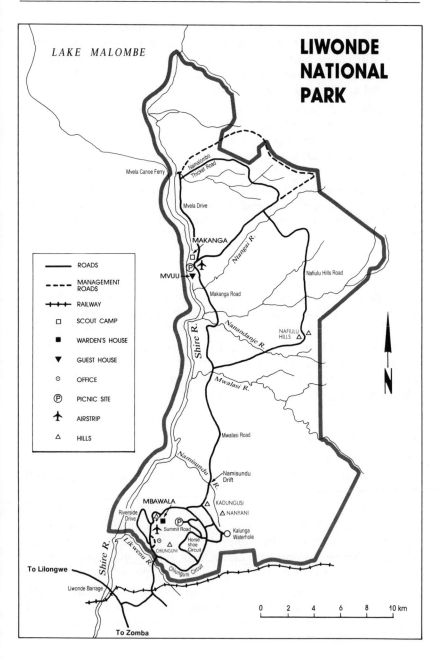

Shire Princess, a sizeable boat based at Kudya Discovery Lodge, offers the tourist trips up and down the river lasting approximately three hours. Rift Lake Charters, which is based near Club Makokola on the lakeshore, also offers motorboat cruises on the river followed by a bush walk and an overnight stay at Mvuu Camp.

In addition, the m.v. *Sunbird* often takes tourists on an approximately six-hour trip from Club Makokola along the lakeshore, through Lake Malombe and downriver to Kudya Discovery Lodge at the southern end of the park. Enquiries regarding these trips can be made at Club Makokola (see page 171). (For accommodation details see page 163.)

Petrol is not sold at Mvuu Camp, nor are shopping facilities available. However, a filling station and some shops do exist in Liwonde itself and at the township across the Kamuzu Barrage spanning the Shire River.

Access

Liwonde National Park lies 120 km from Blantyre (via Zomba), approximately 100 km from Nkopola Lodge on the lakeshore, 245 km from Lilongwe and 46 km from Zomba. (See route section, page 121.)

The Kamuzu Barrage township lies about a kilometre or so north of the turnoff to Liwonde township, just off the main Lilongwe/Zomba road. A signposted untarred road leads past the shops to the Kudya Discovery Lodge on the west bank of the Shire River.

Lengwe National Park

Conveniently situated only 74 km south of Blantyre, Lengwe's 887 km^2 area is the most northerly region in Africa in which the rare nyala antelope is found.

Formerly a reserve, the park was proclaimed in 1970 in order to provide increased sanctuary for the dwindling population of nyala, and with the provision of water-holes their numbers have increased considerably. These shy creatures can be seen at close quarters in the early morning or late afternoon at viewing hides overlooking the water-holes.

Among the other animals to be seen in the park are bushbuck, sable, kudu, warthog, bushpig, hartebeest, impala and duiker as well as Livingstone's suni and the rare blue monkey. Buffalo, lion and leopards have occasionally been spotted.

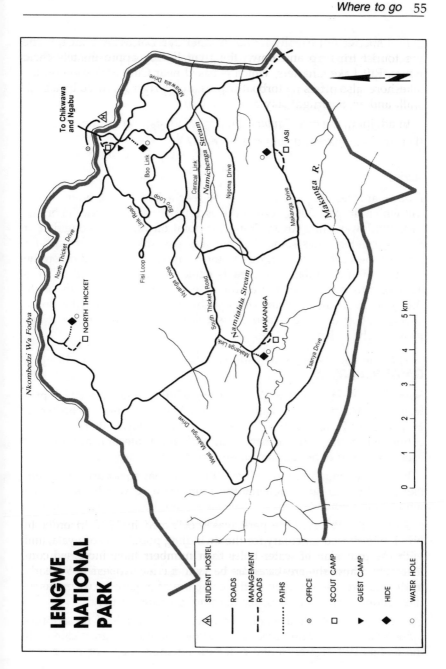

LENGWE NATIONAL PARK

STUDENT HOSTEL

ROADS

MANAGEMENT ROADS

PATHS

OFFICE

SCOUT CAMP

GUEST CAMP

HIDE

WATER HOLE

To Chikwawa and Ngabu

Nkombedzi Wa Fodya

North Thicket Drive

Boo Link

Boo Loop

Link Road

Fisi Loop

Nyanga Loop

South Thicket Road

West Makanga Drive

NORTH THICKET

Mbawala Drive

Caracal Link

Namichenga Stream

Ngoma Drive

Makanga Drive

JASI

Makanga R.

Namidala Stream

Makanga Link

MAKANGA

Tsanya Drive

0 1 2 3 4 5 km

Bird species not usually found in other parts of Malawi include the gorgeous bushshrike, the barred long-tailed cuckoo and the black and white flycatcher.

Visitors are able to walk freely in the park as long as they are accompanied by a game scout.

The park may be closed to visitors at the height of the rainy season. (For accommodation details see page 152.)

Access

From Blantyre, the park can easily be reached within an hour via the M8 which drops 1 000 m down the escarpment and crosses the bridge over the lower Shire River. From this point onwards the condition of the road deteriorates somewhat but it is passable by saloon cars for most of the year. However, during the rainy season, depending on the severity of the rainfall, the area is liable to flood. In addition, it is advisable to use the second entrance to the park, which leads off to the right from the road to Nchalo. The distance between the police checkpoint at the bridge and the second entrance to Lengwe is approximately 20 km.

GAME RESERVES

Some very scenic areas and interesting wildlife populations are protected by Malawi's four game reserves, Vwaza Marsh, Nkhotakota, Majete and Mwabvi. Animal densities are much lower than those encountered in the national parks but with the protection afforded by each reserve, it is hoped that these densities will increase.

Being very much less developed than the national parks, they are likely to hold an attraction for the more intrepid wildlife enthusiast who is prepared to "rough it". For this reason the reserves are not very popular with tourists and in some cases they have not been visited for many months.

Tracks that may have existed within the reserves are not regularly maintained and in many cases are likely to have disappeared. Walking in the reserves is permitted in the company of a game scout but as in the national parks, his presence does not guarantee safety.

Hunting is prohibited within the reserves. All types of fire are forbidden outside the camp areas and visitors should take great care with the disposal of cigarettes and matches. Firearms, dogs, or other pets will not be allowed into the reserves. Permits are necessary for entry into the reserves and these may be obtained from the Chief Wildlife Officer, Department of National Parks and Wildlife (see address page 183).

Vwaza Marsh Game Reserve

Fairly close to the Nyika National Park, the much lower-lying reserve comprises marsh and woodland, rocky hills, floodplain, the scenic Lake Kazuni and Zaro Pool.

Some of the animals that have been sighted in the reserve include elephant, buffalo, hippo and many species of antelope. The reserve's birdlife is rich and diverse and offers the photographer plenty of opportunity.

At the lake itself there are many waterbirds to be seen while a wide variety of riverine and woodland species are attracted to the vicinity of the Luwewe River, making a walk along its banks extremely re-warding. An alternative haven for birds is the floodplain alongside the South Rukuru River, which drains Lake Kazuni.

Unfortunately, Vwaza Marsh is also home to the tsetse fly, which is likely to plague the visitor even in his vehicle. The fly is extremely resistant to sprays and lotions and inflicts a painful bite which in some recorded cases has been infected, resulting in sleeping sickness (see p. 139). Note that the hot dry season, from about October till the onset of the rains in December, can be unpleasantly hot.

A tented camp overlooks Lake Kazuni but its proximity to the S49 can detract from the peacefulness of the surroundings.

The reserve can be reached by following the S85 from Rumphi in the direction of Nyika. Ten kilometres past Rumphi, take the left turn onto the untarred S49 and drive for about 19 km to the reserve entrance. The road is likely to be impassable to ordinary saloon cars during the rainy season. (For accommodation details see page 155.)

Nkhotakota Game Reserve

Lying on the Rift Valley's western escarpment, the reserve is set in hilly terrain covered with miombo woodland and some evergreen forest.

Animals that inhabit the reserve include elephant, zebra, buffalo, hippo, crocodile, lion, leopard, hyena and a number of species of antelope.

The Bua River runs through the reserve and attracts the *mpasa* or lake salmon on its spawning run in the early part of the dry season. The river also attracts the *sanjika*, a smaller cousin of the *mpasa*. A permit is required for those intending to fish in the river (see section on angling, page 82).

Access to the Reserve is from the M10, which runs through it from Nkhotakota to Lilongwe via Mbobo and Ntchisi or via Kasungu. The road is mostly untarred and may give problems during the wet season. There is no road network in the reserve. (For accommodation details see page 155.)

Majete Game Reserve

Lying on the west bank of the lower Shire River to the south-west of Blantyre, the reserve's large residents include elephant, kudu, sable and waterbuck and nothing much else of interest to the average tourist.

Something that is of interest, however, are the Kapichira Falls, which lie adjacent to the reserve's entrance at the end of the road leading from Chikwawa. These are the first of the Shire River's 64 km stretch of cataracts encountered by David Livingstone in his attempt to reach the lake by riverboat. They forced him to dismantle his boat and have all the parts carried by porters on foot to the upper section of the Shire past the northernmost cataracts before he could reassemble his boat and continue on his way.

The falls are also a favourite fishing spot for anglers in search of tiger fish.

Majete can be reached by taking the M8 from Blantyre until Chikwawa and then turning right through the village and continuing for about 23 km. (For accommodation details see page 155.)

Mwabvi Game Reserve

Lying in the most southerly region of Malawi, some 130 km from Blantyre, the Mwabvi Reserve lies in hilly terrain interspersed by sandstone ridges and rocky gorges.

Animals of interest that may be spotted in the reserve include black rhino, leopard, hyena and a number of species of antelope. The evergreen thicket holds particular promise for birdwatchers.

The reserve is extremely isolated and somewhat difficult to reach, the roads leading up to it being in bad condition and in some cases non-existent after the floods of 1989. The chances of the guard at the gate speaking any English are remote and apart from having to produce an entry permit, the visitor is very much left to his own devices. (For accommodation details see page 156.)

Forest Reserves

The Malawi government has set aside a number of forest reserves with the intention of protecting some important areas of indigenous forest. These include the Mulanje, Zomba, Dedza, Ntchisi and Dzalanyama reserves which, although they are not likely to harbour the larger mammals, may offer the bird enthusiast some rewarding sightings.

Visitors may walk freely on some of the paths and tracks in the reserves and camping is permitted in certain places. (For accommodation details see page 149).

OTHER PLACES OF INTEREST

Likoma Island

Together with its much smaller sister island, Chizumulu Island, Likoma is set entirely within Mozambican waters. Lying across the lake from Chintheche on the western shore, the island, 8 km long and 3 km wide, was allocated as Malawian territory in the 1950s when the Portuguese and British split the southern portion of Lake Malawi between the two powers.

Development began in about 1886 when Will Johnson and Chauncy Maples, two members of the Universities Mission to Central Africa of the Anglican Church, settled on the island after deciding to establish it as the headquarters of the Anglican Church in Nyasaland.

Their endeavours resulted in the construction of an impressive cathedral, the same size as Winchester Cathedral in England. Known as St Peter's Anglican Cathedral, the church, complete with stained-glass windows, was built between 1903 and 1905 on the spot where suspected witches were once burnt alive.

It was designed by Frank George, an English architect who was later appointed archdeacon. As time passed, the building deteriorated markedly until in 1970, the Life President, Dr H. Kamuzu Banda visited the island and offered a generous donation in order to initiate restorative work. The cathedral now stands completely restored, although reduced in height and decoration, but still as incongruous as it always must have seemed.

Likoma Island was the headquarters of the Anglican Church in Malawi until the 1940s. The Anglican missionaries proved to be so zealous in their work of educating the local population that at one time the island's inhabitants had the distinction of being 100 per cent literate. Likoma Island was apparently the only settlement in Africa that could claim such a high literacy rate.

Compared with Chizumulu, Likoma is barren, one possible reason being that it lies within the rain shadow of the nearby Mozambican mainland. Despite this, the island is well worth a visit, even if only for its cathedral and for the fact that it seems so remote from the negative aspects of twentieth century life. The visitor may also wish to visit the rural development centre and school.

If you fancy a trip to Chizumulu Island, you could try asking the local chief to organise a ferry across the strait separating the two islands. Interestingly, the waters of the strait have a current which has given rise to the folklore that the spot houses an aquatic monster.

The main form of access to Likoma is by boat although there is an airstrip. The island has a resthouse but very little else in the way of accommodation. If the visitor wishes to stay on the island, one way of doing so would be to sail from a more southerly port to Likoma, alight and possibly camp on the island or stay in the resthouse for the two days and nights it takes for the *Ilala* to return, reboard her and return to one of the ports on the eastern shores of the lake. Alternatively, it is possible to catch the *Ilala* on her northbound journey and alight on the island at midday on Saturday, spend the night on Likoma and return south by boarding the *Mtendere*, which docks at the island at 07h00 on Sunday morning.

Kamuzu Academy

The very last thing you expect to see when driving in the middle of the African bush along a rough dirt road is an elegant edifice in whose construction and maintenance, it is evident, no attention to detail has been spared. Its manicured lawns and man-made lake further accentuate the Academy's estrangement from the surrounding environment. To complete the picture, you only need to catch sight of a boater-hatted student!

About 32 km east of Kasungu in the Central Region (along the S54), stands this monument to classical education. Known as "the Eton of Africa", Kamuzu Academy was inspired by the Life President, Dr H. Kamuzu Banda's determination to provide the very best in education for Malawi's people.

The Academy, which was created along the lines of a British public school, is intended to attract Malawi's elite pupils with a view to forging the future generations of Malawi's leading citizens.

Only those with the highest marks, regardless of background, are selected by public examination and region of origin to study at the Academy where, at the express wishes of the Life President, great emphasis is placed on the study of classical languages and the moulding of the student in an attempt to create the whole or complete person. It is interesting to note that at the Academy, tribal custom is forsaken and girls compete on an equal basis with boys.

Built at the expense of His Excellency the Life President, the Academy's fine buildings, with their stately lawns, lake and playing fields, were opened in 1982.

Kamuzu Academy is situated at Mtunthama ("place on the hill") near a national monument area containing the *kachere* or wild fig tree under which His Excellency the Life President was said to have studied as a young boy.

Both the national monument area and Kamuzu Academy are open to visitors but it is best to phone the Academy (see page 185 for telephone number) prior to travelling there, in order to make an appointment to tour the school.

Livingstonia Mission

Established in 1894 as the third attempt to found a mission station away from the hazards of malaria, Livingstonia Mission is today the centre of a small, but thriving and hardworking community.

It is well worth a visit, if only for its splendid situation on the edge of the 6 km^2 Khondowe Plateau at the foothills of the Nyika Plateau overlooking the lake and, in the distance across the lake, the view of the magnificent Livingstone Mountains. In addition, the mission and all that has been created around it are monuments to the zeal and industry of the trail-blazing Scots missionaries.

The buildings of the mission station, with its technical workshops, church, post office, clocktower and old homestead that strongly resembles the style of a typical Scottish house, have all been declared national monuments. The church, which is still incomplete, contains a stained-glass window depicting David Livingstone and his loyal helpers.

The mission was set up by the Scot Dr Robert Laws with the aim of providing a well-balanced industrial education focusing on medicine, theology, technology and agriculture. The station's isolation forced it to become self-supporting and one of the fruits of its determination to survive – a recently restored hydro-electric plant – was built in 1905, giving it the distinction of being the first mission site in Central Africa with an electrical supply.

The refurbished Old Stone House that forms part of the mission was the second residence of Dr Laws and was built in 1903 of stone blocks hewn from a nearby quarry. A small museum and shop selling handicrafts have been established for the benefit of visitors. Visitors are able to stay at the old guest house on the mission (see page 157 for contact details).

The road from the lakeshore up to the plateau was built by Dr Laws in 1905. The 16 km untarred road, known as the Gorode, features a nerve-wracking drive with 20 hairpin bends climbing a height of some 600 m. At the very least the drive can take up to an hour to negotiate and possibly more, depending on weather conditions. During the rainy season, the road has been closed on occasion due to mudslides. Needless to say, the drive is recommended for four-wheel-drive vehicles only, particularly during the wet season. To give an idea of the tightness of some of the bends, vehicles that are larger than those of standard four-wheel-drive dimensions have to negotiate the bends in more than one movement.

The Manchewe Falls, where the Chitimba River plunges 300 m, are situated just off the top of the road. Just behind the falls is a cave, a visit to which may be of interest to the more daring sightseer. The cave is said to have been used as a refuge during times of tribal strife. Superb views of the Livingstonia Mountains 80 km across the lake make the area an excellent site for a picnic. Not far from the homestead is the 100 m long Khondowe Rock Shelter which features several rock-paintings.

The mission can be reached from inland via the tarred M1 from Mzuzu, which bypasses the road to Rumphi. An untarred turnoff from the M1 to the left (D10) cuts across to the untarred Livingstonia Road, saving the driver from having to travel some 26 km on dirt. Once you have reached the Livingstonia road, turning right off the D10, look out for Nchenachena, a village with a resthouse where one may stay if accommodation at Livingstonia is unavailable.

Mua Mission

Also known as the White Fathers' Mission, Mua is situated in the Central Region close to the Balaka/Salima road (M17) just before the turnoff to Monkey Bay. The mission was founded in 1889 by the first representatives of the Catholic Church to enter Malawi.

The mission is known for its woodcarvings, produced by local apprentices who have been taught at the mission's workshops. Father Boucher, a French-Canadian priest, has been the major force behind the teaching of this craft to local artists. The carvings mostly depict aspects of Malawian culture and history.

3 WHAT TO DO

Malawi is not only likely to appeal to the general tourist who enjoys a spot of game-viewing combined with a few days' relaxation at the lake. The country also offers much to those with special interests.

This chapter describes areas that are likely to hold a special appeal for walkers and hikers, those who fancy some birdwatching, anglers, watersport enthusiasts, souvenir hunters, tropical fish enthusiasts and those who enjoy seeking out rare and elusive orchids.

FOR WALKERS, HIKERS AND CLIMBERS

Those who enjoy walking will benefit from visits to most parts of Malawi. However, for those who prefer a little climb over rather varied terrain or maybe even something a bit more demanding, the best places to visit are the Zomba Plateau and Mulanje Massif.

Zomba Plateau

All who have visited Zomba Plateau will agree that it is a magical place, which offers so much that the visitor will be drawn to return there again and again, each time finding something new. The plateau forms the north-eastern end of the Shire Highlands stretch, which in its south-westerly corner terminates in the Blantyre region.

Over 100 years ago the town of Zomba with its majestic plateau attracted the first settlers and the area might have formed the focal part of the fledgeling country had the settlers not decided that it was too close to the passing slave-route and that it harboured too many dangerous wild animals for comfort.

Despite gaining the distinction of becoming the capital of Malawi and then losing the title to Lilongwe, Zomba and its plateau have for some fortunate reason never attracted excessive commercial exploitation nor lost their heavenly aura of peace and beauty. Nowadays, the plateau stands guard over the small town which, in housing the main university campus, has quite appropriately become the intellectual centre of Malawi.

Gazetted as such in 1913, Zomba Plateau is the oldest forest reserve in Malawi. Its potential as a forest reserve was recognised as early as 1895 when the first plantations of cypress and Mulanje cedar were planted. The reserve's total area of 47 km², which includes both the outer slopes and the plateau, is today planted with the relatively fast-growing conifers of Mulanje cedar, cypress and Mexican pine.

The plateau actually forms a basin that is ringed by a number of peaks: Nawimbe, Malumbe, Chiradzulu, Chivunde, Mulunguzi and Chagwa. In the west, the plateau's face offers spectacular views overlooking the Shire Valley and the Kirk Range of mountains far in the distance. To the south, with the town of Zomba at the foot of the plateau, the visitor can enjoy magnificent views of the Mulanje Massif, soaring to 3 002 m from the surrounding Phalombe Plain with Lake Chilwa to the east.

The stunning views from the plateau's rim are just one of a host of bonuses for the visitor to Zomba. The plateau also houses a variety of features that will prove to be never-ending sources of delight for the walker and hiker, the trout fisherman, the horserider, the camper and even the standard car-bound tourist.

The plateau contains two dams: Chagwa Dam near Chagwa Peak and Mulunguzi Dam lower down on the plateau. The former contains black bass while the latter is stocked with trout from the trout ponds on the plateau. Those keen on fishing (see section on trout fishing, page 85) can obtain a licence at the Ku Chawe Inn hotel.

There are a number of pretty waterfalls, including Mandala Falls which drains into Mulunguzi Dam, Williams Falls just off the circular road, and a number of smaller falls all set in lush, verdant surroundings where ferns, lichens, mosses, creepers, orchids and other wild flowers abound.

Wildlife on the plateau includes leopard, hyena, hyrax (dassies), otters and monkeys while the more common birds include the saw-wing swallow, mountain wagtail, Livingstone's loerie, white-tailed crested flycatcher, fiscal shrike, stonechat, wailing cisticola and Bertram's weaver. Birds of prey include the augur buzzard, the eagle owl, the long-crested eagle, the white-necked raven and the ubiquitous African pied crow.

The plateau is easily accessible from the centre of Zomba, where a signpost indicates the beginning of the winding 7 km "up" road, so called because only traffic going up to the plateau is allowed to use the single-lane route. The road is tarred, which facilitates access during the rainy season, though small landslides could complicate matters.

The descent to Zomba from the plateau is by means of a "down" road which only descending traffic is permitted to use. The down road is not tarred but this is countered by the fact that it is wider and not as precipitous as the "up" road. Before the construction of the "down" road, traffic on what is now the "up" road used to ascend and descend the road at closely controlled intervals to prevent the formation of bottlenecks.

As soon as you reach the plateau, you are confronted by the Ku Chawe Inn, a small but popular hotel poised on the edge of the plateau and overlooking magnificent views to the south. From the hotel the road branches into a network of untarred forestry roads, the most widely used being the 24 km circular road which the tourist can follow by car in order to visit the three main viewsites, Queen's View and Emperor's View on the eastern side of the plateau and Chingwe's Hole in the west.

Queen's View was named after the visiting Queen Mother in 1957, while the nearby Emperor's View was named after the former Ethiopian ruler, Haile Selassie, who visited the country in 1964. Chingwe's Hole, in the north-western section of the plateau, lies in a grassy plain. The *chingwe* part of the title means "string" in Chichewa and probably refers to the site's former use as a burial place where bodies were lowered by means of a rope down a 20 m deep fissure in the rocks to a cave. Chingwe's Hole offers panoramic views across the upper Shire trough to the Kirk Range in the west. On a clear day Lake Malombe, at the southerly end of Lake Malawi, may be visible.

Although the circular road is in good condition during the dry season, when the tourist should allow himself an hour and a half to complete the circuit, it could become impassable to ordinary saloon vehicles during the rains. Likewise, if on ascending the circular road it is obvious that mist and cloud are seeping into the plateau area over its rim it is best to call off your intended trip as the chances of obtaining good views in such weather are slim.

Apart from a trip by car round the plateau via the circular road there is quite a wide variety of walks that can be followed. These have been documented in a fairly dated booklet called *Zomba Mountain – A Walker's Guide* by H.M. and K.E. Cundy, copies of which may be available from the hotel or from Montfort Press, the publishers (see page 185 for address).

The NFPS (National Fauna Preservation Society of Malawi) as it was previously known (now the Wildlife Society of Malawi) also published two very useful booklets entitled *Zomba Plateau – Mulunguzi Nature Trail* and *Chingwe's Hole Nature Trail*. Both booklets should be obtainable from the hotel or from the Wildlife Society itself (see page 183 for address).

At the entrance to the hotel a kiosk offers quite a wide range of wooden curios. Also on sale are a variety of fruits in season such as strawberries, rhubarb, guavas and the Himalayan raspberries which grow wild on the plateau and are worth trying when they are harvested in the months of October and November. The Zombo potato, a tiny new potato which is usually on sale all year round, is delicious when roasted or baked and particularly worth buying.

Across the road from the kiosk is a Forestry Department hut, constructed out of Mulanje cedar, which contains a scale model of the plateau and points of interest on it.

Just along the ridge from the hotel is a riding stable that hires out horses and ponies for rides on the plateau.

Mulanje Massif

When looking at the towering bulk of Mulanje from a distance one gains the impression that God, not satisfied with the creation of an enormous lake, thought He would leave yet another expression of greatness by creating Mulanje.

Lying in Malawi's south-eastern corner, bordering on Mozambique, and rising to a height of 3 002 m from the surrounding, unremarkable Phalombe Plain, Mulanje, Central Africa's tallest mountain, looks like an afterthought that is not a little bit out of place.

The massif is topped by 20 peaks rising to heights of over 2 005 m and includes the neighbouring Mchese Mountain.

A variety of footpaths lead to the massif's five plateaux from the road encircling its foot. To reach the plateaux rock-climbing is not necessarily involved but for those who are reasonably fit, the fairly steep paths are easy to negotiate. The walker's level of fitness will determine times taken for ascent, which at the most should not take more than five to six hours.

The more enthusiastic mountaineer can take out his or her frustrations on a number of challenging peaks. Manga (1 906 m), the cone-shaped

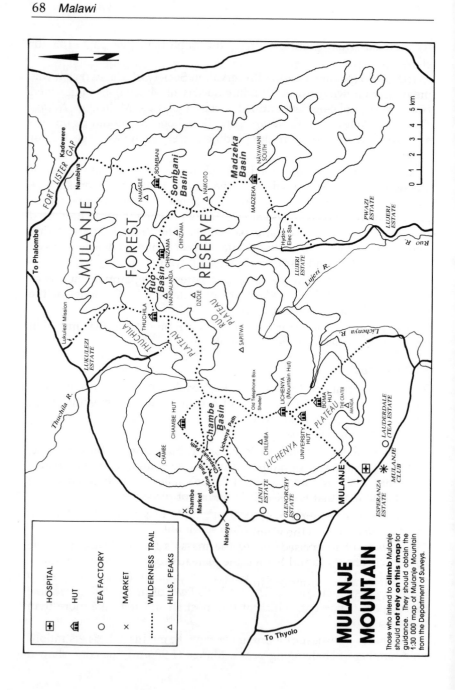

MULANJE
MOUNTAIN

Those who intend to **climb** Mulanje should **not rely on this map** for guidance. They should obtain the 1:30 000 map of Mulanje Mountain from the Department of Surveys.

peak above Mulanje town, was first ascended in 1956 and has been climbed relatively few times since, as routes are difficult and unprotected. Chambe's magnificent west face (2 556 m), which towers over the Phalombe Plain, has one very severe Grade 5 route involving some 400 m of roped climbing. A first ascent was made in 1977 with a roped climb of 1 700 m at a difficulty rating of Grade VI A1. It is said to be the longest rock climb in Africa.

Those wishing to climb the mountain should contact the Mulanje Mountain Club (see page 183 for address details) as members are always willing to help with advice.

The neighbouring forest-clad mountain of Mchese is separated from the main massif by Fort Lister Gap, through which a road runs. Superb views can be seen from the gap, which is named after the military settlement established there in 1893 to observe and control slave-trading traffic that passed through the area to its ultimate destination in Zanzibar. The ruins of the fort, which was abandoned in 1903, are still visible. The graves of two officials who were buried there lie in the vicinity of the Fort. One of these officials, Gilbert Stevenson, was the cousin of the famous novelist, Robert Louis Stevenson.

Mchese has been climbed a number of times but there is no obvious path or track that may be followed. Climbers should therefore be wary of losing their way especially on the descent.

Some of the streams draining the plateaux and basins are stocked with trout and even though the trout are on the small side, angling in these superb surroundings will more than make up for their lack of size. (See section on trout fishing, page 85.) The streams that are said to offer the most rewarding sport are Likhubula stream at the eastern foot of the mountain, Chapaluka stream in the Chambe Plateau basin and the Lichenya stream on the Lichenya Plateau.

All streams on the mountain are said to be safe for bathing but extra care should be taken in the vicinity of waterfalls and rapids. In addition, caution should be exercised against getting out of your depth in waters that can be very cold and have slippery rocks underfoot.

The different landforms of Mulanje have resulted in a variety of plant habitats, ranging from dense tropical rain forest with varieties of balsam and begonia found in the ravines, to the ericas or heathers and giant blue lobelias that can be found on the taller sections of the plateaux. Being older landforms, these sections possess the characteristics of a cooler, more temperate climate than could normally be expected in a place like Malawi. A number of iris species are also found, the most obvious of which is the indigenous Mulanje iris, as well as the waxy, flame-coloured red-hot poker. The exotic staghorn lily, white with a blue tinge, is often visible clinging to exposed rocky outcrops during the latter part of the dry season.

In spring, the white and yellow helichrysum "everlasting flower" can be found carpeting the ground while the white, pink-tinged Whyte's sunflower, which is unique to Mulanje, is found in amongst the rocky areas. To contrast this, Mulanje's wetter regions harbour a wide variety of ferns, mosses, and creepers.

The visitor should note that it is an offence to pick flowers on Mulanje as they are all protected.

Mulanje is home to the Mulanje cedar, which reaches heights of 45 m and is said to be the world's finest softwood. Larger specimens can reach ages of 200 to 300 years. The species is fairly slow-growing, taking between 60 and 70 years to mature.

Because the plateau is not accessible by vehicle, timber that is felled is often sawn by hand near the felling site before being carried down the mountain. As a walker on the mountain you may come across the arresting sight of a wood carrier with an enormous load precariously balanced on his shoulders. To maintain his balance and that of his load, he has to do a kind of measured jog that is between a fast walk and a run. One can only wonder as to how fit these barefoot carriers must be.

The wood of Mulanje cedar gives off a delightful fragrance and this most probably makes it resistant to termites, although it is highly in-flammable and the younger trees in particular risk being destroyed by fire during the dry season. Carved chests in a variety of sizes made out of the scented wood are easily available for purchase on the street in Blantyre. Check for cracks in the wood, though, which indicate that it has been carved before being allowed to dry out sufficiently.

Wildlife on the plateau is not easy to spot but animals such as red duiker, bushpig and bushbuck, leopard and porcupine certainly do exist and the visitor is extremely likely to see the rockrabbit or hyrax.

When planning a trip to Mulanje note that if the rains are to be avoided, a visit should coincide with the months between April and December. The best times for climbing are said to be from mid-April to the end of July. The southern reaches of the plateau tend to be wetter for a longer part of the year than its northern reaches which lie within the mountain's rain shadow and have a longer dry season.

There is always a danger of mist and fairly rapid cloud buildup, particularly in the wet season, when visibility can be seriously and dangerously impaired. Any hint of adverse weather conditions should be well noted as it is fairly easy to get lost under such conditions. This is even more so during the "chiperone", which is the name for the very wet mist that can invade the massif between May and August for days at a time. The chiperone can also occur during the rainy season, when it is hardly distinguishable from drizzle and low cloud.

Conditions during the wet season render many paths impassable, sometimes necessitating the use of ropes for fording streams and rivers that might be in flood. In such weather it would be wise to organise the services of a guide. The visitor to Mulanje should also be aware that from one moment to the next a trickling stream can turn into a raging torrent as rain upstream collects in a wall of water on its way down the mountain.

To avoid hazardous weather conditions during the wet season, rock climbing on Manga Peak should be undertaken between August and October while Chambe should be climbed between May and October.

Daytime temperatures are cool between May and August and night-time temperatures do not preclude the possibility of frost. Even snow has been sighted on Sapitwa at this time. From August to November, hot and dry conditions expose the walker and climber to the risk of severe sunburn.

Those wishing to spend the night off the mountain can stay at Mulanje Club, which has camping facilities with good amenities (see accommodation details, page 167). However, for those who would prefer to intersperse walks and climbs with a night on the mountain there are six forestry huts run by the Department of Forestry for the use of walkers and climbers. (See accommodation details, pages 153, 156.) These are situated on Lichenya and Thuchila plateaux and in the Chambe, Ruo, Sombani and Madzeka basins and are clearly pinpointed on the 1:30 000 map of Mulanje available from the Map Sales Division of the Department of Surveys (see addresses, page 184).

The Mulanje Mountain Club maintains its own equipment in lockers in the huts but access to this equipment, which includes camp beds, mattresses, lamps, cooking and eating utensils, is only available by prior arrangement with the secretary (see page 183 for address). The club offers the use of these facilities to reciprocal members or parties accompanied by a member.

The forestry huts themselves should be booked in advance by writing to the Principal Forest Officer, Mulanje (see page 185 for address) with the party leader's name, address and telephone number, with the number and names of all the party members and their names and addresses and dates of the party's intended use of the huts. The cost of overnight use of the huts is extremely reasonable and payment can be made either in person to the Forestry Office or by post.

It should be noted that permission to camp within the Forest Reserve should be obtained from the Principal Forest Officer. Under normal circumstances, camping is prohibited in the dry season months of June to November.

There is no need to undergo the discomfort of lugging gear up the mountain as superfit porters are usually available for hire near all the main paths to the plateaux, and if not, can be organised by the Forest Officer. Their rates of hire are laid down by the Department of Forestry and it is advisable that every effort be made to conform to these rates.

Each porter should be able to manage a weight of up to 16 kg. If the porters will be required to spend the night on the mountain then both food rations and the use of a blanket should be provided. Guides are also available by prior arrangement with the Forest Officer.

Members of the Mountain Club recommend that, to assist the Forest Officer in discharging his rescue operation duties, he is supplied with information regarding the date of climb, party leaders and names of party members, details of proposed trip and estimated time and date of return. These details should be left at the Likhubula Forestry Office or at the Mulanje Police Station. Parking spots and the recommended paths for ascending Mulanje are indicated on the map of Mulanje.

In case of accident or emergency, basic first aid equipment such as bandages, elastoplast, antiseptic ointment and painkillers should be included in your luggage. Other essential items are a map, compass, whistle, spare food supplies, a torch with an extra supply of fresh batteries, and a warm sleeping bag and anorak.

It is possible to reach the massif from Blantyre via two roads. The shorter of the two, which runs through Midima, is partly gravel and is unlikely to be in good condition during the rains. The single-strip tarred road running via Thyolo is longer by 16 km but is likely to hold more scenic appeal for the tourist as it traverses the rolling tea estates.

From Thyolo (where you should consider visiting the Thyolo Club for a wonderful pot of tea, among other things) the road continues for another 40 km to Mulanje. Just 2 km short of Mulanje is an untarred road branching off to the left which leads to Likhubula, just over 9 km away, after joining the circular road leading round the base of the massif. Note that during the wet season, the Likhubula drift may be impassable while heavy rains may make the road itself temporarily impassable.

Chambe village is just under 2 km on the same road from Likhubula and a further 13 km travelling leads to Thuchila and Likulezi. A distance of 11 km separates Likulezi and the village of Phalombe, at which junction one can choose to turn left and join the untarred S40 for 60 km to Zomba, although this probably would necessitate the use of a four-wheel-drive vehicle. Alternatively, turn right to join the road heading through the Fort Lister Gap between Mulanje and Mchese. This road (S43) may be in poor condition and four-wheel-drive vehicles are recommended even during the dry season while their use is regarded as essential during the rains.

At the village of Mkhulambe you should turn right if you wish to return to Mulanje and travel on the untarred D147 for approximately 31 km before joining the single-strip tar road that heads back to Mulanje. Just off this road, some 7 km from Muleza, lies the path to Lujeri.

A book has been written on the massif for those who require much greater detail on its walks and climbs. Entitled *A Guide to the Mulanje Massif* it was written by Frank Eastwood and published by Lorton Communications, Johannesburg, in 1979. A number of copies of a recent reprint were made available to the Mountain Club from whom the book can be obtained. Alternatively, try contacting the publishers in South Africa (see page 185 for address) to enquire whether they may be of assistance in obtaining a copy.

Walks around Blantyre

Blantyre is cradled by three mountains: Ndirande (1 612 m) to the north-east, Michiru (1 473 m) to the north-west and Soche (1 533 m) to the south. The summits of Ndirande, which because of its shape is known as the "sleeping man mountain", and Michiru Mountain are accessible by car, while Soche must be climbed.

Ndirande Mountain

Ndirande's summit has two viewsites, one of which is known as Kamuzu View. The viewpoint overlooks Coronation Dam which supplies the city of Blantyre with drinking water, and offers a superb view of the city, flanked by the Soche and Michiru mountains.

Ndirande's summit is accessible via an untarred road that may present conventional cars with problems during or just after the wet season. From Blantyre, follow one of the two main roads out of the city (Glyn Jones Road or Haile Selassie Road), which join just before the clock-tower roundabout. The left-hand turn just before the roundabout leads into the Chileka road. This should be followed for a distance of just under 2 km before turning right into the Ndirande ring road and travelling for about a kilometre. At this point a dirt road leads off to the left through the township of Ndirande before beginning its climb up the mountain.

After the hustle and bustle of Blantyre the mountain seems utterly deserted and completely peaceful. Pine plantations, ferns and wild flowers make it strongly reminiscent of Zomba Plateau.

The visitor should be warned that there have been reports of break-ins in parked cars that were left unattended at either of the viewsites.

Michiru Mountain

The bulky mass of Michiru stretches a few kilometres to the north-west of the city. Its summit, complete with picnic sites and cleared camping areas, can be reached via a road that runs through the township of Chilomoni. This road is in fair condition during the dry season but it is recommended that only four-wheel-drive vehicles attempt to negotiate the route during the wet season.

A variety of trails, differentiated in terms of their difficulty and the length of time it takes to complete them, have been laid out in what is known as the Michiru Mountain Conservation Area. The easiest and shortest walk takes only half an hour and follows the course of the Mikwawa River. The next two trails concentrate on an area at the base of Michuru and take in the local hyena caves, where hyena can sometimes be spotted towards sunset. Trail 4 leads to Michiru Peak after a two and a half hour ascent, while Trail 5 runs along the summit of the mountain.

Animals that can be sighted from the trails include duiker, bushbuck, reedbuck, klipspringer, baboon, mongoose and vervet monkey, together

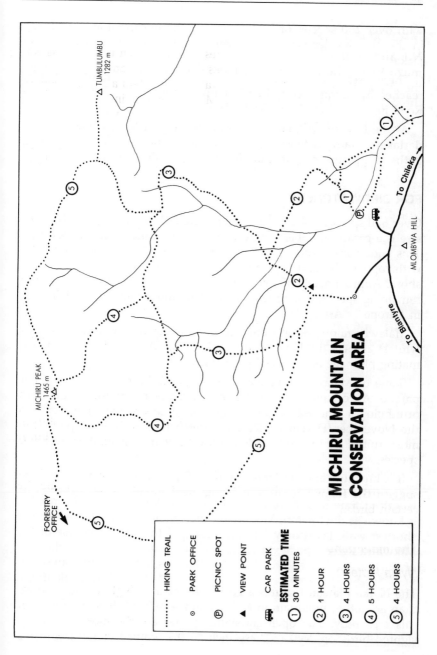

MICHIRU MOUNTAIN
CONSERVATION AREA

TUMBULUMBU
1282 m

To Chileka

MLOMBWA HILL

To Blantyre

MICHIRU PEAK
1465 m

FORESTRY
OFFICE

.... HIKING TRAIL

⊙ PARK OFFICE

Ⓟ PICNIC SPOT

▲ VIEW POINT

🚍 CAR PARK

ESTIMATED TIME

① 30 MINUTES

② 1 HOUR

③ 4 HOURS

④ 5 HOURS

⑤ 4 HOURS

with over 200 species of birds. Some of the nocturnal animals living in the area are leopard, serval, wildcat, civet, genet, porcupine and jackal.

The conservation area with its educational centre and office can be reached by taking Michiru Road, signposted to the right off Glyn Jones Road just after the Mount Soche Hotel.

At the time of writing, the Wildlife Society of Malawi had just undertaken a fairly extensive project which involved clearing viewsites, paths and roads and generally improving facilities on the mountain.

FOR BIRDWATCHERS

Over 600 species of birds have been recorded in Malawi, which for its size is a greater number than can be found in most African countries. This wide variety can be attributed to Malawi's varied natural habitat with topography and vegetation ranging from mountain top to lakeshore. Approximately 530 species are thought to breed in Malawi, the remaining species encountered being vagrants or migrants originating in Europe or Asia.

Malawi's rainy season from December to April (during the northern winter) attracts the long-distance migrants, while birds in distinctive mating plumage are especially conspicuous.

Some of Malawi's indigenous birds spend the dry season in other parts of Africa, although the dry season can be rewarding for the keen ornithologist who wants to fit in a bit of game viewing. However, it is the November/December/January stretch that is likely to prove the most fruitful for the birdwatcher, with the chance of sighting over 400 species.

In a brochure entitled *Birds of Malawi* R.J. Dowsett and Michael Gore suggest the following areas as being ideal situations for sightings of certain birds:

The mountains

Nyika Plateau

The Nyika Plateau features a greater number of high-altitude species than any other mountain in Malawi and several of them are found in this area only. The open-grassland species are the most commonly sighted birds on Nyika. These include the wattled crane, Denham's bustard and red-winged francolin, which are mainly confined to this area in Malawi.

Evergreen forest, which can prove to be the most interesting habitat on the Nyika, harbours the attractive cinnamon dove, bar-tailed trogon and starred robin. Other rarer species that may be spotted are the white-chested alethe, the olive-flanked robin and Sharpe's akalat. These birds are difficult to spot as they may be feeding high in the forest canopy but a measure of patience might well be rewarded.

Forests surrounded by a belt of bracken briar contain species such as mountain and churring cisticolas and streaky seedeater. The bracken and open grassland, with their wide variety of seasonally flowering plants, are likely to attract such sunbirds as the greater double-collared and red tufted malachite.

The Chowo Forest region on the Zambian border, with its extensive trail system, is likely to contain more varieties than the Juniper Forest, which can also be rewarding.

Ntchisi Mountain

The fine Ntchisi Mountain forest, which is within fairly easy reach of Lilongwe, attracts quite a few of the high-altitude forest birds, in addition to several species typical of miombo woodland.

Thyolo Mountain

A few of the bird species that are absent from the north are attracted to the Southern Region mountains. These include the extremely rare bronze-naped pigeon, green-headed oriole and Natal thrush.

Zomba Plateau

Zomba Plateau features a nature trail in the Chingwe's Hole area where the Thyolo alethe and black-headed apalis can be found. The white-winged apalis can be seen in riverine forests at lower altitudes near Zomba.

The fairly short nature trail that runs along the Mulunguzi Dam and stream and parallel to the road returning to the dam traverses a variety of habitats. Species that can be spotted include the water-associated saw-wing swallow and mountain wagtail, while those to be seen in the riverine evergreen forest include the Livingstone's loerie or turaco and white-tailed crested flycatcher.

Species that are fairly evident in the grassland and bracken briar are the fiscal shrike, stonechat, wailing cisticola and the yellow Bertram's weaver.

Birds of prey present on the plateau include the augur buzzard and long-crested eagle, while the white-necked raven and African pied crow are extremely obvious.

Rocky hills

Malawi's rocky hills, as distinct from its mountains, often prove to be rewarding vantage points from which to spot birds of prey, as either passing migrants or as breeding residents. Many rocky hills are to be found in the Dowa and Dedza areas as well as in the Monkey Bay region of the lakeshore. These regions typically contain the black eagle and lanner and peregrine falcon, while the black stork, mocking chat, rock cisticola and large striped pipit may also be spotted.

Lakeshore forest

The Nkhata Bay/Chintheche stretch of lakeshore supports evergreen forest akin to eastern Africa's coastal forests. The most accessible section of this area is the small Kalwe Forest on the main road near Nkhata Bay, where Cunning's akalat may be spotted in addition to the interesting green coucal, red-capped robin and blue-mantled crested flycatcher.

Miombo woodland

Brachystegia species are dominant in the deciduous ("miombo") woodland that once covered a large part of the southern portion of Central Africa and still harbours a number of species unique to this habitat.

An interesting characteristic of miombo woodland is the loose collections of individuals of many different species that may feed and travel together. A prime example of this habitat is to be found in the Dzalanyama Forest Reserve south-west of Lilongwe, which is easily accessible for a day's visit.

Most of the miombo bird species occur here and the birdwatcher has every chance of spotting the rare Stierling's woodpecker and olive-headed weaver. The elusive lesser seedcracker can sometimes be seen near evergreen trees along the woodland streams.

Ntchisi Mountain's evergreen forest is popular with many Dzlanyama miombo bird species such as the olive-headed weaver.

Wood hoopoes and helmet shrikes are widespread in degraded areas of miombo woodland in several regions.

Mopane woodland

Found mainly in the Southern Region, this deciduous woodland is widespread in Liwonde National Park bordering the south bank of the Shire River, between Lake Malombe and the Kamuzu Barrage.

Birds that are commonly seen in this habitat include the red-billed and crowned hornbills, long-tailed starlings and white-browed sparrow weavers.

Liwonde National Park's mopane and acacia woodlands house the attractive Lillian's lovebird, a species unique to this area within Malawi. Pel's fishing owl is more commonly seen or heard here than in any other locality in Malawi.

Thicket

Lengwe National Park has remnants of dense deciduous thicket that are likely to be more interesting to the bird-watcher than any other thicket in the country. They contain crested guineafowl, barred long-tailed cuckoo, black-and-white flycatcher and gorgeous bush-shrike.

Thicket species that are more widespread include the African broadbill and Boehm's bee-eater, a very attractive species with a limited distribution.

Acacia and mixed woodland

Open woodland occurs most noticeably in the Central Region as well as in some lakeshore areas and in the extreme south, for example Lengwe National Park. This area features the yellow-billed hornbill, the only species unique to this particular habitat in Malawi.

Mixed woodland, once dominant in the Lilongwe area and now centred on the Lilongwe Nature Sanctuary, features a wide variety of species. These include a few red-winged warbler, most likely to be seen in the thick undergrowth below acacias, and the giant eagle owl, which might be spotted on the larger thorn trees by the more fortunate birdwatcher.

Bamboo clumps within associated thickets sometimes house pied mannikins and African broadbills, which might be seen displaying at dusk here.

The Lingadzi River, which flows through the sanctuary, attracts size-able colonies of spotted-backed weavers to its banks as well as the occasional white-backed night heron and the African finfoot.

Gardens

Malawi's urban gardens offer the observer a delightful variety of col-ourful birds such as the lilac-breasted roller, the little bee-eater, the green loerie and the impressive scarlet-chested sunbird. Often spotted at the end of the dry season and at the start of the rains are two visitors to Malawi, the paradise flycatcher and the African hoopoe. Indeed, between November and March, some residents even complain at the cacophony of magnificent birdsong that punctually rouses them from their slumbers at literally the crack of dawn, usually 5.15 am.

Lake Malawi

The more interesting varied habitats that support birdlife along the lakeshore are in the Monkey Bay/Mangochi area and the Salima lake-shore district. Few bird species are actually supported by the lake itself, although Boadzulu or Bird Island and Mumbo Island house huge nest-ing colonies of the white-breasted cormorant.

The African fish eagle is said to be at its most dense concentration, anywhere, in the southern lakeshore area, and large numbers of golden and brown-throated weavers are supported by reedbeds. The collared palm thrush can be spotted in thickets under palm trees, the mottled spinetail near baobab trees, and the palm swift in the region of palm trees.

Rivers and wetlands

Pools and small rivers are particularly likely to attract large numbers of birds during the dry season. A striking example is the hamerkop, which is the only member of a family unique to Africa and Madagascar.

The giant and half-collared kingfishers often inhabit well-wooded rivers and rocky stretches attract long-tailed wagtails. The ornithologist will be rewarded by visits to the Bua River in Nkhotakota Game Reserve, Kapichira Falls and Mpatamanga Gorge on the lower Shire River in the Southern Region.

During the August/November season Eurasian shorebirds, as well as numerous species of herons, egrets and ducks, are attracted to Lake Chilwa, which lies to the east of Zomba.

Smaller wetlands such as Vwaza Marsh Game Reserve, Lake Kazuni in the Northern Region, Mpatsanjoka River near Salima in the Central Region and near the Kasinthula Research Centre in the south offer rewarding birdwatching experiences.

Large colonies of the beautiful carmine bee-eater nest in the sandbeds and cliffs overlooking the Shire River near Chikwawa in the south and are at their most evident during the dry months of October and November.

A suggested birdwatching itinerary

For the birdwatcher with two or three weeks to spend travelling in Malawi, local ornithologists have suggested the following programme:

From Blantyre travel to Lengwe National Park and spend one night at the camp, visiting Kasinthula and the Chikwawa area if sufficient time is available. From there travel to Zomba Plateau, using the Ku Chawe Inn or campsite as a base for visits to Lake Chilwa. After Zomba head for Kudya Discovery Lodge on the Shire at the Kamuzu Barrage. Spend some time driving around the park and/or on the river, taking in a three-hour boat trip on the *Shire Princess*.

After a possible detour to the lakeshore, you could head for Lilongwe, which can be used as a base to visit the Dzalanyama Forest Reserve, Lilongwe Nature Sanctuary and Salima. Head for Kasungu and spend a day and night there before travelling north to Mzuzu, taking in a possible stopover at the resthouse at Chikangawa on the Viphya Plateau. Mzuzu can be used as a base for visits to Nkhata Bay and Kalwe and Nkwadzi Forest Reserve before heading for Nyika National Park (at least four nights) and then back to Lilongwe or Blantyre.

All localities mentioned in this section are shown on the 1: 1 000 000 map of Malawi, which is available from the Department of Map Surveys.

As with other wild animals, birds are at their most active during the cooler hours of the early morning and late afternoon, although they may still be seen during the day. Forest species are busiest when it is hottest outside the forest.

FOR ANGLERS

With 30 per cent of its surface area under water, Malawi offers the angler and tropical fish enthusiast a rich and varied fish fauna.

Apart from Lake Malawi, where about 250 of an estimated total of between 500 and 1 000 species of fish have been described so far, fish habitats include the large marshy and lagoon areas to be found around Lakes Chilwa and Chiuta and in the lower Shire Valley, particularly in the region of Elephant Marsh.

The big fish angler will have to look elsewhere, however, for despite Malawi's abundance and variety of fishing grounds, most of the fish fauna is classified as small and therefore requires the use of light tackle only.

The visitor who is keen to do some angling should pack in his baggage a light spinning rod, a fixed spool reel loaded with a 2,5 kg (6 lb) line and a variety of spinners. The visitor keen on tiger fishing requires a heavier tackle (see below), while the tourist interested in trout fishing should pack light fly fishing tackle if he is to visit the trout fishing areas of Nyika National Park, Zomba Plateau and Mulanje Massif during the season, which runs from 1 September to 30 April.

Apart from the pleasure to be gained merely by fishing, the angler in Malawi scores double in that he can enjoy his sport in a variety of locations, most of which are blessed with magnificent scenery.

Tiger fish

A species that is much sought after by freshwater anglers in Africa is the tiger fish which, in Malawi, is found at the foot of the Kapichira Falls (formerly the Livingstone Falls), an area that has been protected from deforestation and cultivation, making it particularly scenic especially early in the morning, which is the best time for tiger fishing.

The falls are adjacent to the southern boundary of the Majete Game Reserve some kilometres north of Chikwawa in the lower Shire Valley. The largest concentrations of tiger fish are found here, although it is also found throughout the Shire River south of the falls.

Fishing at the falls area requires slightly heavier tackle than that described above to catch the 4,5 to 7 kg fish which are often encountered. A popular tackle combination for nabbing these larger fish is a 5,5 to 7 kg line with a wire trace and big silver lures or wooden plugs.

The best time for tiger fishing is during the dry season (May to early November), when the water is likely to be clearer.

To reach the falls from Blantyre follow the scenic Chikwawa Road, which in 16 km descends 900 m to the floor of the valley. The road continues along the valley floor, which is less than 100 m above sea-level and can prove to be very warm during the hot season, until it reaches Kamuzu Bridge across the Shire River. Just across the river, turn right for the falls through Chikwawa township, approximately 1 km after crossing the river.

The 18 km track leading to the falls and the southern boundary of Majete Game Reserve can be tricky during the wet season, when four-wheel-drive vehicles are recommended, as the road contains a number of steep drifts. Be prepared for the drifts to be impassable, as they were during the floods of 1989. However, members of the Angling Society manage to follow the track in ordinary saloon cars during the drier months. In favourable conditions the time taken to travel from Blantyre to the falls is one and a half hours.

If you wish to combine a game-viewing trip with a fishing excursion, comfortable chalet accommodation is available at Lengwe National Park, approximately 22 km south of Chikwawa along the M8. Chalet accommodation is also available at the Sucoma Sugar Estate at Nchalo, 28 km south of Chikwawa along the same road. In both cases prior booking arrangements should be made (see section on accommodation, page 155). In fact, a number of employees at the Sugar Estate are keen anglers and members of the Angling Society and would be willing to give the visitor advice on fishing tackle and techniques.

Tsungwa

This thick-set, deep-bodied fish is mainly found in the quiet, palm-tree and papyrus lined banks of the upper Shire River near Mangochi and Liwonde or around rocky coves and islands in Lake Malawi where the *tsungwa* is more scarce but can grow to much larger sizes of over 2 kg and 40 cm in length. This is particularly the case in areas that are off the beaten track, for instance around Likoma Island.

In rocky coves or around islands where the rock shelf drops to the sandy bottom at depths of 6–9 m, a sinking spinner will often be intercepted before it reaches the bottom. However, takes normally occur on the first half to one metre of retrieve. The best spinner to use under these circumstances is a blue spotted or plain silver Mepps No 4.

Specimens of up to 1 kg can easily be caught in the rivers and weedy patches on the lakeshore. The most effective spinners in these areas are the Effzetts and blue-spotted Abu Droppens.

Mangochi's Fisheries Department office hires out boats when they are not required for official duties and staff members are willing to advise the fisherman on appropriate tackle and best fishing locations. Lakeshore hotels also hire out boats but there is a lack of reliable information at hand on where to fish. In this case, the angler should rely on his own "water sense" and concentrate on finding the types of areas described above.

Lake salmon (mpasa)

This member of the carp family, which closely resembles the salmon (but is unrelated) in habits, appearance and fighting ability, is unique to Malawi.

Specimens of up to 3 kg can be found at pools in the Bua River in the Nkhotakota Game Reserve in the Central Region where elephant trails are followed to get from one pool to the next. This river has the largest run of *mpasa* during the height of the season, which occurs from April to June. However, angling in the reserve is limited to holders of a special permit, obtainable from the Department of National Parks and Wildlife in Lilongwe. Other rivers that contain *mpasa* are the Luweya, Lufira and North Rukuru in the Northern Region.

Any small silver lure, the most effective being the Abu Droppens or small Effzetts, will attract the *mpasa* during the spawning run from the lake up the rivers. The dates of the spawning run vary from river to river but it generally occurs towards or just after the end of the rainy season (April to June).

At the height of the season, anglers have no trouble in catching over a dozen *mpasa* averaging 1,5–2 kg in weight during a day's fishing. The *mpasa*'s smaller relative, the *sanjika*, which averages 500 g in weight, is even more rewarding for the angler, who can expect to catch a dozen of these for each *mpasa* caught.

Catfish and yellowfish

The largest fish to be found in Lake Malawi are those belonging to the African catfish family, specimens of which have been recorded as measuring up to 1,5 m in length and weighing up to 30 kg.

The catfish and yellowfish can be caught in Lake Malawi's tributary rivers when legering with pieces of crab as bait. Such legering on the shores of Lake Malawi at night can yield catfish as well as eels weighing up to 5 kg though under these conditions the most likeliest catch is of softshell turtles sometimes weighing up to 20 kg.

Using legered ox heart and heavy tackle, large *vundu* (another catfish), often over 15 kg, can be caught in the lower Shire River south of the Kapichira Falls.

Black bass

These are found in dams on the tea estates in the Mulanje/Thyolo region, where fishing is by permit only. Worm bait used in these dams can also result in catches of large *Tilapia* species.

Rainbow trout

The three main locations for trout fishing in Malawi are at the Nyika, Mulanje and Zomba plateaux.

The three dams on Nyika Plateau, plus a number of streams, offer the most rewarding fly fishing in the country. Accommodation on the plateau is available at Chelinda Camp (see page 154), which is within the National Park, providing the visitor with the opportunity of some game-viewing at the same time.

Zomba Plateau's best trout fishing can be enjoyed in beautiful surroundings at the Mulunguzi Dam, fed by the fairly fast-flowing Mulunguzi stream, in the midst of cool pine forest. The dam is stocked from the trout ponds further up on the plateau where fingerlings are reared before being released into the dam. However, the fish are on the small side owing to the water's purity and the scarcity of natural food.

Accommodation on the plateau is available at the splendidly situated Ku-Chawe Inn (see page 163) or at the campsite.

To cap a trout-fishing visit to Zomba, the trout angler is sure to enjoy a visit to Zomba Fishing Flies, a small fly-tying factory situated at the foot of the mountain at the northern exit of the town on the left-hand side of the road. Apparently one of the four largest fly-producing concerns in the world, the factory holds over 2 000 samples.

Mulanje offers the opportunity of catching fish in streams draining the plateaux, which can be reached by a number of footpaths. These include the Likhubula stream at the foot of the mountain, the Chapaluka stream in the Chambe Plateau basin and the Lichenya stream on the Lichenya Plateau.

The first of several attempts to stock the streams with trout was made in 1905, but none were successful until 1935, when a population explosion forced the authorities to remove all trout fishing restrictions. Nowadays, although trout can still be caught, they are likely to be on the smaller side, but the peaceful, timeless beauty of the trout-fishing surroundings more than make up for this lack of size.

The open season on Mulanje is from 1 September to 30 April, with the streams remaining low in volume generally until the first rains, in November.

The officer at the Forestry Department offices at Likhubula sells trout fishing licences and can offer the visitor advice on where to go for the best fishing as well as arranging accommodation at one of the Forestry huts on the plateau. During the wet season it may be advisable to arrange to hire the services of a trout guide.

If you wish to have access to Mountain Club camping equipment in lockers within the huts, you should make prior arrangements by writing to the Mountain Club (see address, page 183). Alternatively, there are camping facilities at the Mulanje Club.

Local experts recommend fly fishing tackle with an AFTM rating of 5 or 6 and the following fly patterns and hook sizes:

Zomba and Mulanje		*Nyika*	
Black Panell	10	Black Zulu	8
Walker's Killer	10	Socdologer	8
Invicta (Yellow)	10	Peter Ross	10
March Brown	12	Mrs Simpson	8
Oliver	10	Oliver (red)	10
Mrs Simpson (evening)	10	Invicta	10
		Phantom/Nyika killer	6

In all cases, only fly fishing is allowed and flies must be tied on single hooks. The season lasts from 1 September to 30 April and daily, weekly and full-season licences are available from the treasury cashiers at Blantyre and Zomba, as well as at Ku-Chawe Inn on the Zomba Plateau, Chelinda Camp office at Nyika National Park and at Likhubula Forestry Department offices at Mulanje.

FOR WATERSPORT ENTHUSIASTS

Windsurfing, parasailing, dinghy sailing, scuba diving, waterskiing, pedaloes, canoes – all these water sports can be enjoyed in Lake Malawi's waters. The major hotels on the lakeshore, Club Makokola, Nkopola Lodge and Livingstonia Beach Hotel, provide facilities for these activities. In addition, trained staff, and in some cases, qualified instructors are available to help the novice watersport enthusiast to derive the full benefit from his or her endeavours.

Scuba diving safaris can be arranged from Club Makokola and Nkopola Lodge. The aquarium-like waters off the rocky shorelines of the southern portion of the lake make this sport particularly rewarding. At present, divers will not be supplied with air unless they can produce a diving certificate. However, there are plans for a qualified instructor to conduct diving courses. Those who wish to join the scuba safari or courses should contact Rift Lake Charters (see useful addresses, page 184) with regard to booking arrangements and to ascertain whether their own equipment should be brought into the country or whether equipment will be supplied.

Weather

Any sporting activity that is carried out on the lake should be done in the full knowledge that the weather can change suddenly. If a storm begins to brew, waves up to 3 m high can threaten safety. In the light of the above, lifejackets should be worn at all times.

The lake has no tides or currents, but seasonal fluctuations can markedly influence its level. Between the months of March and May the lake is at its calmest. From August to October, the *mwera*, the prevailing south-easterly wind, greatly increases in velocity. Just before the rains, between October and December, the wind changes direction, becoming more northerly. At this time of year it is known as the *mpoto*. Wind direction and velocity is variable and unpredictable during the rainy months of December to January, but by February it again becomes south-easterly.

Lake Malawi marathon

Lake Malawi is a superb venue for the annual Lake Malawi marathon, which is apparently the longest lake marathon of its kind, 560 km. It takes place over a week, usually in July, and a number of different classes of boat, including windsurfers, are eligible for entry.

Teams of helpers follow the progress of the competitors from the shore and camps are set up at the various overnight stops.

Those interested in further information regarding the marathon should contact the Department of Tourism in Blantyre (see page 184 for address).

Sailing clubs

There are two sailing clubs operating on the lake: the Salima Yacht Club, operating from Livingstonia Beach Hotel, and the Ndirande Sailing Club, based in Blantyre but operating from Nkopola Lodge.

Visitors who may require further information regarding sailing on the lake should contact the Ndirande Sailing Club commodore (see useful addresses, page 183).

FOR SOUVENIR HUNTERS

One of the pleasures of visiting Malawi, especially for the souvenir hunter, is to be gained from the abundance of curios that are found on sale both within the commercial centres and on the sides of the road.

Prices are cheapest in areas that are off the beaten track, while street salesmen in the cities and larger towns, and, of course, the established curio boutiques, are more in tune both with the amount of spending money that is likely to be dispensed by tourists and their lack of knowledge regarding the local value of curios.

Ivory

Good quality ivory is readily obtainable but to guard against poaching, the collection and sale of ivory is strictly regulated by the Malawi government. In the light of this, the tourist should not purchase ivory unless the seller can produce a trophy dealer's licence and provide an official receipt.

Those who wish to take ivory out of the country should first obtain an export permit from the Department of Parks and Wildlife (see address on page 183). Failure to conform with the above requirements could result in confiscation of illegal ivory as there is every possibility that it will be detected at the various points of exit from the country.

There is a wide selection of expertly carved ivory objects available from vendors, ranging from small items of jewellery to the very attractive ebony and ivory chess boards complete with carved figures. However, the ivory should be examined closely to ensure that its characteristic grain is visible. (Hippo tooth and bone are completely smooth in appearance and free of any grain.)

In the interests of wildlife conservation, more and more countries are actively discouraging the importation of ivory and it is worth checking whether your country of origin is supporting this strategy before buying any ivory.

Export permits for ivory goods are at present obtainable only from the Department of National Parks and Wildlife offices in Murray Road, near the Old Town in Lilongwe. All ivory to be exported must be taken to the office together with sales receipts and tusk numbers, before a permit will be issued.

Soapstone

Top quality soapstone, ranging from a dark mottled green to a pale grey/green, is imaginatively carved to depict human figures, busts and heads, as well as animals, insects and fish. The soapstone, which is mined in the Ntcheu district in the Central Region, is heavy though soft in texture, and if dropped is quite likely to be chipped or damaged.

Malachite

Dark and lighter green-tinted malachite is available in the form of necklaces and bracelets off the street while the curio shops have more sophisticated items made out of this attractive mineral, which can be highly polished.

Wood

Wood carving seems to be the most ubiquitous of Malawi's crafts and a wide range of items will be found at the lakeshore and in the main centres. The two most characteristic types of wood used are African mahogany, which is lighter in colour and of larger dimensions than ebonywood, which is much blacker and, as it is slow-growing, more difficult to come by.

Other hardwoods are often used for carvings and the tourist will be amused to see roadside salesmen openly polishing the items with black and red shoe polish. The items are nevertheless attractive and are protected by such an application of polish. In the case of salad bowls and utensils the visitor should note that the polish soaks into the wood and does not contaminate food. Nor can it be washed off – indeed, these items should rather be cleaned by the application of a small amount of cooking oil, which further conditions and seals the wood. The purist who wants to make sure of what he is buying should check the item by scraping its underside with a blade to see if any polish or stain is removed.

The visitor should also be on the look-out for hairline cracks in wooden items, which indicate that the wood has been carved before being allowed to dry out.

Apart from a wide variety of nick-nacks that are ideal as gifts, some of the more interesting items available in wood include the "chief's chair", many examples of which can be seen on the side of the road between Zomba and Liwonde, outside the PTC and Kandodo shops in Old Town, Lilongwe and outside the main PTC shop in Blantyre. There is also a wide variety of interesting masks ranging in size and weight from a few kilograms to those weighing around 50 kg, and some massive, solid wooden busts which are extremely impressive.

A visit to the Gangecraft curio centre at Bvumbwe is worth while for those who can't be bothered to bargain and prefer to do without the charm of the street-sellers. Gangecraft is a centre for the mass-production of items, most of which are exported. Here skilled craftsmen are employed under supervision and items are likely to be of a quality superior to those found in the street. The visitor can ask to be shown around the premises where he will see the wood being cut to size, then hand carved or turned on a lathe before being finished and polished.

Simply designed, practical furniture is made by local craftsmen out of feather-light palmwood, which despite its lightness is extremely strong. Tables and chairs made out of palmwood are ideal for use in the garden. These can be seen for sale on the side of the road near Machinga between Zomba and Liwonde.

Attractively carved chests ranging in size from small jewellery boxes to large linen chests are made out of Mulanje cedarwood, which gives off a delightful fragrance for quite some time after the wood has been carved. These are usually available outside the main PTC in Blantyre. The carvers' workshops are situated at the entrance to Chilomoni township, which can be reached if one follows Glyn Jones Road from the

Mount Soche Hotel in a north-westerly direction. The road curves into Chilomoni Ring Road, which should be followed for just over a kilometre before the workshop signs become visible on the roadside.

Basketwork and grass

Basketwork is evident everywhere in the form of shopping, wastepaper and laundry baskets, and even tables and chairs. Good use is made of grass, which is woven into a large variety of mats (the best designs are usually to be seen on the Mangochi–Liwonde road), trays, hats, table mats, picnic and shopping baskets, Moses baskets, and imaginative copies of toys in the form of cars, helicopters, boats and trucks.

Pottery

Pottery is available in a variety of forms, the most basic being cooking, water and food storage pots, which can prove to be attractive plant containers. There is a large selection of these pots in Lilongwe market, and some are available on the side of the road between Zomba and Blantyre.

A large selection of imaginatively worked, reddish-brown clay figurines in a variety of poses is usually available off the street in both Blantyre and Lilongwe.

The two largest potteries are those at Dedza and Malindi. They both produce a wide range of oven-proof items for the table, together with cups, saucers, mugs, ashtrays, vases and other containers. Each pottery uses its own distinctive glazes and styles. Some of these items are sold in shops in the main centres but they are generally cheaper if bought directly from the pottery – which, in both cases, will prove interesting to visit.

Malindi is on the eastern shore of the lake just north of Mangochi. On reaching Mangochi one should head for the bridge across the Shire River and continue for 6 km before taking the turnoff to Malindi, which is 12 km further along an untarred road that can become impassable during the wet season.

Malindi Potteries have a retail shop in Mangochi itself, tucked away in a clearing on the left-hand side of the main road once one has turned off the Liwonde–Monkey Bay Road. However, there is a much wider range of items available at the pottery itself.

Dedza Pottery is reached by taking the turnoff into Dedza from the Lilongwe side on the M1 from Lilongwe to Blantyre. There is another entrance into Dedza from the Blantyre side but the road from the Lilongwe entrance is much shorter if one is pressed for time.

Weaving

Macoha, the Malawi Council for the Handicapped, provides paid employment for handicapped people in its workshop just outside Limbe, near Blantyre. The workshop produces a variety of attractive woven cotton mats together with a number of other items such as rugs, oven gloves, hammocks and wall hangings.

These articles are available in a number of shops in the main centres but if one is in Blantyre it is worth setting aside an hour or so to visit the centre, which has its own retail section. The centre can be reached from Blantyre by taking the Kamuzu Highway to Limbe, and continuing through the centre of Limbe along Livingstone Avenue, which joins up with Churchill Road. Turn right at this point onto Churchill Road and continue along it past the Limbe Country Club on the left until it becomes Midima Road. The workshop is a couple of kilometres past the level crossing on Midima Road and is clearly signposted on the right-hand side.

Printed fabrics

Virtually all the branches of PTC and Kandodo, many of the Asian shops and all David Whitehead sales outlets stock colourful Java prints in lengths of material which can conveniently be used as wraps.

Notes on bargaining

As in most other countries, local street salesmen will take the opportunity to ask a much higher price of obvious tourists than would normally be asked of a resident. One method of bargaining involves making a counter-offer, roughly half the price asked. You can choose to use this method if it is not very important whether the sale is concluded or not.

In some cases, the visitor will be amused and astounded when the salesman states his next price as being just a kwacha or so more than half-price, or even accepts the price. If the salesman feigns disbelief and returns with a price that is slightly less than his first price, and if you are fairly keen to purchase the item, then increase your price by degrees to a level that is approximately a quarter less than the first price mentioned.

At this point you can choose to walk away and one of two things will happen: either the salesman will accept the reduced price or he will lose interest himself and walk away knowing he can get a better price somewhere else. If the latter happens and you truly desire the item in question, then you will have to swallow your pride and call the salesman back and accept his price with maybe just a small discount.

Curio salesmen at the lake and outside of the larger centres are far keener to meet the potential buyer halfway than those plying their trade in more urbanised areas, who are likely to be tougher in their bargaining methods. Of course, the established shops have their fixed prices and are not open to discounting unless a large number of items are to be bought or if the items in question are somewhat defective or inferior in quality.

It is worth remembering that many street salesmen will accept clothing and other items in lieu of money.

FOR ORCHID LOVERS

According to Isobyl La Croix, author of the specialist publication *Malawi Orchids*, Malawi's more than 400 orchid species constitute one of the largest listings of orchids in Africa. This fact, together with the country's great topographical variety, is likely to give much pleasure to those visitors whose main quest is orchids. Generally speaking, the best time for orchid hunting is November–April, while the most rewarding places are the Nyika Plateau and Mulanje/Zomba areas.

Of the terrestrial species, over 280 have been listed, while a total of over 120 epiphytic species are now known to be found in Malawi, the majority of which have been observed to be very local in their occurrence. It has also been noted that they may be found in abundance in one area but absent from another which seemingly has similar conditions. To add complexity to the variety of habitats, orchids may also be found on one tree in a particular area but not on another of the same species close by.

FOR TROPICAL FISH ENTHUSIASTS

The 3 000 km long split in the earth's surface known as the African Rift Valley houses seven lakes, of which Lake Malawi is the most southerly.

Lake Malawi vies with two other large lakes in the chain, Lake Victoria and Lake Tanganyika, for the distinction of having more kinds of fish than any other lake in the world. Apart from an annual fish harvest of some 40 000 tonnes that provides over 16 000 people with a livelihood, the lake is distinguished by the fact that it is home to the stunningly coloured *mbuna* or rock fish, which has attracted the keen attention of aquarists worldwide.

Although overall more than 350 endemic species have been identified and their characteristics documented, the lake is reasonably estimated to be home to more freshwater fish species (between 500 and 1 000 species) than are found in all the waters of both Europe and North America.

While the *mbuna* are found at many different locations in the lake, their existence in one particular locality – around Cape Maclear in the south – has been protected by the formation of the Lake Malawi National Park (see page 48). Said to be the only freshwater breeding area in the world declared a world heritage site by Unesco, Cape Maclear and its associated islands offer the visitor an opportunity for some spectacular underwater "game viewing". In many cases just a mask and snorkel are needed to appreciate the variety of different coloured *mbuna* and observe their complex feeding and breeding patterns.

It must be stressed that the waters extending 100 m from the shorelines included in the National Park are protected areas. Watersports, motorboats and fishing are prohibited in these areas and action will be taken by park officials should they find anyone transgressing this ruling. The removal of live *mbuna* from these waters is also considered a serious offence.

Within the boundaries of the park are areas that can be classed as traditional fishing grounds for some of the villages in the region. Instead of banning fishing outright, legislation has limited it to specific spots from where villagers are allowed to pull in their *chilimila* nets (open-water seine net) with catches of migratory pelagic fish. This ensures minimal disturbance of the breeding and feeding patterns of fish communities endemic to the various zones that make up Lake Malawi National Park.

Tropical fish enthusiasts throughout the world know the brightly coloured cichlid fishes of Lake Malawi as the *mbuna*, the name given them by the Tonga tribespeople of the Nkhata Bay area. Without exception, the *mbuna* are small in size, the largest being no longer than 15 cm.

Apart from their amazing variety of colours, the *mbuna* hold a fascination for marine biologists because of their "adaptive radiation". This is the ability of a group of closely related animals to evolve a variety of modifications and achieve specialist "niches" for themselves. In the *mbuna*, adaptive radiation has influenced feeding mechanisms and depth preferences, allowing a number of different species to exist within the same area without directly competing for food sources.

As is typical of endemic Lake Malawi cichlids, the *mbuna* are mouthbreeders, meaning that fertilisation of the eggs takes place in the female's mouth where they then hatch, and where they are kept until they are released one by one to fend for themselves. Once they are ready to be released the female deposits them in rocky crevices where they are able to hide from predators.

The *mbuna* are largely found in rocky areas where they display the characteristic of never venturing away from their chosen type of habitat. This has the effect of isolating the different species, and only a few species of *mbuna* occur throughout the lake.

Certain types of *mbuna* have been imported from other parts of the lake and introduced into habitats where they have become established. This has led to a World Wildlife Fund sponsored study by the Malawi government's Fisheries Department to examine such aspects as competition for food and breeding space between exotic and endemic species, and their relative rate of spread.

Although vast numbers of *mbuna* live in the rocky areas of Lake Malawi's shores, the more spectacular species are found in the zone on the lake floor where the rocks meet the sand. This is particularly so in crevices and caves where there is a sandy bottom and a roof of rock.

According to the authors of the book *A Guide to the Fishes of Lake Malawi National Park* (see Bibliography, page 193) probably the best viewing site in the whole park is Mitande Rocks, a reef jutting off the south-west point of Thumbi Island West. This area features an underwater nature trail made up of six numbered markers at various points around the rocks. Another underwater nature trail is to be found at Otter Point, where ten numbered markers are linked by white stones. A detailed description of the trails together with the species of fish to be found in these areas is available in the abovementioned book. Unfortunately the condition of the trails has deteriorated over time, but the Wildlife Society of Malawi has undertaken to rehabilitate them.

To support the *mbuna*'s extreme popularity with aquarists around the world a thriving export trade in the fish has sprung up. Since the mid-

1960s, when the first consignments were caught by butterfly net and exported to Europe, sophisticated methods of harvesting this colourful earner of foreign currency have evolved to the point where skilled divers using specialised equipment seek out their prey in all corners of the lake.

A variety of means of transport are used to ensure that these unusual fish safely reach the Tropical Fish Holding Centre just outside Salima in the Central Region. Here they are carefully examined and sorted before being held in tanks until they are re-examined prior to shipment to Kamuzu International Airport and then on to Europe and North America. It is possible for tourists to visit the fish centre (see page 183 for address details).

4 HOW TO GET THERE

TRAVELLING TO MALAWI

There are two ways of travelling to Malawi: by air or by road. This section concentrates on how to get there and the formalities and practical considerations involved in getting into the country.

By air

Malawi's only international airport is Kamuzu International, situated 23 km outside Lilongwe, the capital. Although fairly small in size it is regarded as one of the cleanest and most efficient of the African airports.

Major air links exist between Malawi and South Africa, Zimbabwe, Zambia, Tanzania, Mozambique, Kenya, the United Kingdom, France and the Netherlands, among others.

By road

Most visitors entering Malawi by road will enter either from Zambia via the Chipata/Mchinji border posts or from Zimbabwe via Tete in Mozambique and the Mwanza border post in Malawi. Malawi's border posts are open around the clock.

Via Zambia

Although they are permitted entry into Zambia if issued with a visa, South Africans should be warned that their government has advised them not to visit the country in case of harassment by Zambian police.

There are many roadblocks on the stretches of road from the Victoria Falls to Lusaka and then on to Chipata/Mchinji and the attitude of the policemen manning these roadblocks can be unpredictable. Should they suspect you of being a South African spy (even if you are the holder of a non-South African passport) they may consider detaining you temporarily or at the very least ordering you to unload your vehicle so that it can be searched thoroughly.

It is a good idea to have ready access to a carton or two of cheap cigarettes, some tins of beer, soap, confectionery or newspapers and magazines as these might come in handy for the appeasement of a touchy policeman or soldier.

Bear in mind while calculating travelling time the fact that many Zambian roads are rutted, with large potholes. If you intend spending the night in Lusaka try to ensure that your vehicle is well-guarded, especially if luggage or other items are visible to the passer-by.

Via Zimbabwe and Mozambique

Entry into Malawi by this route, rather than via Zambia, certainly cuts travel time by a long margin. However, because Mozambique is still in a state of war (at the time of writing) entry into Malawi by this route entails taking far greater risks than would be encountered via the Zambian route.

An armed military convoy runs in both directions between Zimbabwe and Malawi each day. The convoy, which is mostly made up of large trucks, is jointly protected by Frelimo and Malawi Army soldiers from possible attack by Renamo guerrillas.

Participation in the convoy entails travelling at fairly high speed, 80–100 km/h, which can be rather demanding considering the very potholed nature of the road on the Tete–Malawi stretch. If you have to stop for some reason, for example a flat tyre, the convoy will wait only 15 minutes before continuing on its way, if necessary without you. Should you be left behind a couple of soldiers may or may not remain with you to provide some protection.

In the light of the above it is advisable to pack your spare wheel where it is most easily accessible in a hurry, also to check before joining the convoy that your wheel nuts can be easily unscrewed. Drivers are advised not to deviate from the road, even to avoid the sometimes very large potholes, as they risk driving over landmines that have been planted on the side of the road. Bear in mind that as recently as July 1989, rocket attacks were launched at the convoy.

Those who wish to join the convoy at the Zimbabwean border should make sure they are at the border post before 06h00 when it is scheduled to depart. It arrives in Tete at about 10h00 and travellers are free to do as they wish until 14h00 when the convoy departs from Tete for the Mwanza border post with Malawi, which it is scheduled to reach at about 17h00.

GETTING INTO MALAWI

Immigration requirements

With the exception of the citizens of the following countries, foreigners require visas on entering Malawi:

Bahamas	Iceland	San Marino
Bangladesh	Israel	Sierra Leone
Barbados	Ireland	Singapore
Belgium	Jamaica	Solomon Islands
Botswana	Kenya	South Africa
Brunei	Lesotho	Sri Lanka
Canada	Luxembourg	Swaziland
Cyprus	Malaysia	Sweden
Denmark	Malta	Tonga
Fiji	Mauritius	Trinidad & Tobago
Finland	Nauru	Uganda
Gambia	Netherlands	United Kingdom
Germany (W)	New Zealand	USA
Ghana	Nigeria	Zambia
Grenada	Norway	Zimbabwe
Guyana	Portugal	

Customs

Duty is not normally charged on visitors' personal effects. This concession applies to items only when they are definitely intended for re-export. No duty is payable on the following items provided they are declared and carried in the passenger's accompanied baggage: 200 cigarettes or 225 g tobacco in any form, 1 quart spirits, 1 litre of beer and 1 quart of wine. This concession does not apply to those aged under 18.

The passenger is allowed to bring into the country a reasonable quantity of consumable goods to meet his immediate needs while travelling within Malawi.

Firearms

To import firearms one should first obtain (well in advance) a valid Tourist Firearms Permit from the Registrar of Firearms (see page 183 for address). These permits are issued only in respect of sporting rifles, including air rifles, and shotguns. Pistols and revolvers are specifically excluded.

The permits are valid for six months from the date of issue and firearms that are imported by the tourist with a valid permit are not subject to duty. If a visitor arrives with a firearm not covered by a permit, the firearm will be confiscated and not released until a permit has been obtained.

Currency regulations

Traveller's cheques and foreign currency notes in US dollars, British sterling and other acceptable currencies are accepted by authorised hotels and banks.

Visitors are not restricted in terms of the amount of foreign currency notes that they may bring into Malawi. If it is their intention to subsequently export this foreign currency when they eventually leave the country, they must, on arrival in Malawi declare the type and total value of the foreign notes they possess and obtain a customs certificate confirming this amount.

If this is not done, on leaving Malawi they will be restricted to the equivalent of Malawi K20,00 and any surplus currency will be confiscated. All exported cash in any currency must be declared at the point of exit. Bear in mind that each passenger is subjected to a polite and superficial body search before departure. Malawi currency notes in excess of K20,00 may not be imported or exported.

Journalists

Journalists are advised to obtain prior clearance before entering the country.

Health certificates

Inoculations for smallpox, cholera or yellow fever are not necessary although they may be required if you intend to pass through an infected area. It is advisable to check on current requirements with your travel agent.

Pets

Visitors may bring their pets with them to Malawi provided that before arrival in the country an import permit is obtained from the Chief Veterinary Officer, Department of Veterinary Services (see page 178 for address).

Visitors must also submit a general health certificate of inoculation against rabies when applying for an import permit, otherwise the animal will not be allowed into the country.

Visitors from countries where rabies is not endemic should realise that rabies is prevalent in Malawi and that bringing their pets into Malawi may result in the animal having to undergo quarantine on returning to their country of origin.

Length of stay

If you have a valid visa or if you don't need a visa, then immigration formalities are minimal if you intend to spend up to 30 days in Malawi. If you wish to spend more than 30 days but less than three months then you need to complete an Entry card before your 30 day Visitor's Permit expires and submit it to the Immigration Offices in Blantyre when applying for an extension. Obtaining permission for such an extension takes no more than half an hour. However, should you then wish to extend your stay after the initial three months, you need to apply for a TRP – Temporary Resident's Permit – at the same Immigration Offices. The procedure takes a little longer – three to four hours – and if permission is granted then you may continue staying in Malawi for no more than six months.

While travelling in Malawi be prepared to show your return air ticket and passport and prove that you have sufficient funds to meet your expenses while in the country.

Airport tax

A departure tax is payable in US dollars by all passengers leaving Kamuzu International Airport. Passengers should pay this before checking in prior to departing. It is also advisable to make provision for this tax when first cashing traveller's cheques, for instance, to avoid any possible administrative complications before leaving the country.

Manner of dress

In accordance with Malawian law, no woman is permitted to wear trousers in public unless required by her religion. Neither are skirts showing the kneecap permitted. If a female visitor arrives at Kamuzu International wearing trousers or a mini-skirt she will be taken aside and asked to buy a length of cloth (*chitenje*) from the airport shop which can be used as a wrap-around skirt. In addition, men with hair longer than the level of the collar may be asked to cut it before entering the country. To avoid embarrassment, it is best to ensure that your manner of dress and length of hair conforms with these requirements before landing in Malawi.

Motor vehicles: licences and insurance

Motor vehicles, caravans and trailers that are legitimately licensed and registered in their country of origin can be brought into Malawi by visitors and used by them for a period of up to six months. As in many other countries, all vehicles are required to hold a minimum third party insurance. Vehicles from South Africa, Lesotho, Swaziland, Zimbabwe and Botswana which have third party insurance from these countries are required to pay only the road tax.

Vehicles registered elsewhere are required to obtain third party insurance, which can be purchased at border posts. Vehicles that are imported into Malawi temporarily are required to possess a triptyque or *carnet de passage*. If the driver is unable to produce this documentation, then a temporary importation permit may be obtainable at the border post.

Foreign driver's licences are valid for six months and those not written in English should be accompanied by a certified, written translation.

Vehicle spares

A limited range of vehicle spares is available in Malawi, and what is available is costly. If spares are not available for your particular type of vehicle they have to be ordered from outside the country, entailing a certain amount of delay.

If you are considering driving to Malawi, you should have a supply of spares for all essential parts and accessories. This supply could include fuses, spark plugs, fanbelts, globes, brake and clutch fluid, funnel, thermostat, a water bottle, engine oil, jump leads, spare set of keys, tow-rope, puncture kit, spare wheel and tubes, jack, spare windscreen wipers if visiting in the rainy season, warning triangles, clutch pressure plate, ignition coil, distributor points, tyre pressure gauge and tyre pump. The tyre pump is a necessity because many garages in the bush (and sometimes even in towns) in Zimbabwe, Zambia, Mozambique and Malawi are unlikely to be able to supply pressurised air.

5 TRAVELLING INSIDE MALAWI

ROAD TRANSPORT
Roads in Malawi

Malawi has a road network totalling over 12 000 km in length. The majority of these roads are untarred, but they allow the driver access to most parts of the country. As in the United Kingdom, Australia and South Africa, the left-hand drive system is in force.

The untarred roads are usually passable throughout the dry season although they are subject to rapid deterioration during the wet season (particularly from December to March) when a large number might become impassable, necessitating the use of four-wheel-drive vehicles.

The Ministry of Works, which is responsible for the upkeep of the roads, does its best to keep in tandem with the seasons and although on-the-spot repairs are carried out during the wet season, only once the dry season begins can roads be thoroughly graded and overhauled.

Even good tarred roads are subject to damage during the wet season when, from one day to the next, all that is necessary for the creation of potholes is a particularly strong downpour and some heavy truck traffic.

The main M1 highway, which runs from Mzuzu in the north through Lilongwe to Blantyre in the south is two lanes wide, as are a number of other major roads. Some of the tarred roads in use are single-strip tar, which is taken to mean that the road is only one lane wide. In certain cases, for instance from Salima to Balaka, these roads have been left to deteriorate with the exception of emergency repairs, probably because they have been earmarked for complete reconstruction sometime in the fairly near future.

Vehicle hire

Only very few vehicle-hire agencies operating in Malawi have branches in all the main centres, at the airports and at a number of lakeshore hotels. Whichever agency you select, always ensure in advance that it will supply a replacement vehicle should you break down in one of the more inaccessible areas. Also find out how long it will take to get a replacement vehicle to you.

On signing a hire contract with any vehicle-hire agency, try and ascertain that essential spares are placed in the vehicle. Also inform the agency of your proposed route and be advised as to whether a four- or two-wheel-drive vehicle is necessary for use on that route. If you mislead the company then you must expect to foot the bill for damages that arise from the vehicle having been used in a terrain for which it is not suited.

Car hire rates in Malawi are relatively expensive but this should be seen in the light of the high cost of spare parts and replacement of vehicles.

The cost of fuel is not included in the rate although vehicles are delivered with a full tank which is filled again at the end of the hiring period so that consumption can be estimated. The rates of hire cover third party liability only. Damage to vehicles is considered the responsibility of the renter but a collision waiver may be purchased in advance as a form of insurance. Despite this waiver, the renter is still responsible for damage that is caused to the vehicle by road conditions, negligence or in the case of accident when no other vehicle is involved. If a breakdown does result from the renter's negligence he will be liable for the cost of recovery and rectification.

Some of the hire agencies offer both self-drive or chauffeur-driven options.

If possible, book your hired vehicle before you arrive in Malawi.

The following companies operate as car hire agencies:

Agency	Location	Phone	Telex
Car Hire Limited	Blantyre	671–495	4557
	Lilongwe	723–812	
	Kamuzu International Airport	760–591	
	Mzuzu	332–622	
Country Car Hire	Lilongwe	721–976	4842
	Limbe	650–775	
	Kamuzu International Airport	760–294	
Hall's Car Hire/ Hertz	Blantyre	633–907	4744
	Chileka Airport	661–219	
	Club Makokola	584–288	4312

Agency	Location	Phone	Telex
	Lilongwe	760–290	
	Kamuzu International Airport	760–046	4787
	Lilongwe (Capital Hotel)	730–444	4892
	Mzuzu	332–122	4467
	Livingstonia Beach Hotel	261–422	4148
Rangers/Budget	Limbe	651–966	4167
SS Rent-a-car	Blantyre	636–836	4531
	Chileka Airport	661–657	
	Lilongwe (Capital Hotel)	733–787	
	Kamuzu International Airport	760–536	
	Lilongwe	721–179	

Public transport

Although Malawi does have a train network, it is not geared for tourist travel. The bus network reaches all parts of the country. Services between the main centres are more regular than those in the outlying areas.

The most efficient and comfortable bus service in operation in Malawi is known as the Coachline and covers the four-hour trip between Lilongwe and Blantyre twice a day.

The terminus for the Coachline in Lilongwe is at the Lilongwe Bus Station in Old Town and at Hall's Car Hire in Anderson Street in Blantyre. A bus leaves from each terminus every morning at 07h00 and reaches its destination at 11h10.

The same bus departs again from that terminus to return to its home base at 16h00, reaching its destination at about 20h10. In Lilongwe an extra scheduled stop is made at the Capital Hotel, and in Blantyre/Limbe the bus collects passengers at the Shire Highlands Hotel.

The service is extremely reliable and almost always on time. No provision is made for unscheduled stops except in case of an emergency. Passengers must book their tickets in advance (see page 184) otherwise they will not be permitted to board the bus. Coachline bookings may be made in Blantyre at Hall's Car Hire and Tours in Hannover Avenue; in Limbe at the Hertz/Coachline offices in the Shire Highlands Hotel; in Lilongwe at the Hertz/Coachline desk at the Capital Hotel or at the Coachline office at the UTM depot.

A less reliable, less comfortable, much slower but certainly more colourful form of service is provided by the Express and Country lines. These buses, together with other lines such as Yanu-yanu, offer access to the more remote corners of Malawi. If you don't mind travelling in generally hot, crowded conditions with live chickens, goats, baskets of fruit and vegetables, and a wide assortment of anything that can be carried, then it's a wonderful opportunity to meet Malawians. Apart from anything else, it is likely that you will encounter only helpful friendliness and polite curiosity on your bus journey.

Some say that the Country-line buses stop under every pawpaw tree, which might account for the slowness of the service. However, these stops are likely to be quite educational, for you may see roadside vendors selling their wares which could be anything from a mouse-kebab to a fried doughnut-type cake or delicious roasted peanuts. (Note: Mouse-kebabs do actually exist! They consist of mice that are caught, generally during a bush-fire, skewered on a long stick and roasted over a fire.)

At the time of writing, UTM, the company that runs the largest public transport operation in Malawi, was considering extending the bus service to the neighbouring countries of Zambia, Mozambique, Zimbabwe and Tanzania.

Destinations and timetables for the various bus services can be obtained from the offices of United Transport (Malawi) in Blantyre and Lilongwe. The offices are open between 7h30 and 12h00 and 13h30 and 17h00 on weekdays.

Hitchhiking

Hitchhiking is permitted in Malawi, though one should realise that it is an unreliable form of travel as the relative lack of regular traffic might make it easier to reach a remote place than to leave it. Remember that the driver offering the lift may not be licensed and his driving skill might consequently be lacking.

The accepted way of hitchhiking in Malawi involves extending your arm horizontally into the road and, while keeping the arm stiff, waving your hand up and down. The driver of a vehicle that can be classed as an "unofficial taxi" may expect payment. This should be discussed before the ride is accepted.

Taxis

Taxis in Malawi are not plentiful or easily recognisable. Although they possess numberplates with red lettering on a white background, this does not automatically distinguish them as taxis because hired vehicles bear the same type of numberplate. In general, the taxis are operated by private individuals and comprise the older vehicle models.

Bear in mind that normally taxis cannot be hailed. However, they can be found operating from bases within the grounds of the major hotels.

Mobile safari operators

As yet, only two legally licensed and registered mobile safari operators practise business in Malawi. *~Correction: see cover page.*

Safari Tours
P.O. Box 2075, Blantyre. Tel: 650-003.
Tariff: High

Based in Blantyre, this company aims at the upper-income bracket tourist who prefers to stay in the comfort of hotels rather than rough it in the bush. The owner has lived in Malawi for several years and has an extensive knowledge of all that is likely to be of interest to the tourist. Small groups are preferred and the needs of special interest groups can be accommodated. Both German and English are spoken by the tour operator.

Land & Lake Safaris
P.O. Box 30239, Lilongwe 3. Tel: 723-459.
Tariff: Medium

This operator aims at the tourist who would prefer to camp in the bush although the facilities of hotels, chalets and lodges are also used.

The company offers a choice of three safaris: a 17-day safari covering the entire country, and two 10-day safaris concentrating on either the northern or southern section of Malawi. Over and above these, special-interest tours such as those involving canoeing, sailing or hiking, can be catered for and tailored to the requirements of a group.

Groups comprise eight people per vehicle with two vehicles some-times being used, depending on the size of the group. Tours are con-ducted in English.

Speed limits

In urban areas speed limits are 48 km/h and 60 km/h, while in country areas it is increased to 80 km/h. In wet weather, it is advisable to keep to low speeds on roads that are in poor condition as this will help prevent damage to the vehicle resulting from driving over potholes. In the national parks, the speed limit is 40 km/h.

Driving etiquette in Malawi

In general, drivers in Malawi tend to drive more slowly than in other countries. This can be construed as a blessing and it is worth while to exercise a degree of patience rather than get hot under the collar.

Note that the use of safety belts is mandatory. Some of the larger centres have zebra-crossings where pedestrians should have right of way. Motorists generally ignore these crossings, however. The best thing to do in such cases is to play it safe and slow down on approaching a zebra-crossing. If you do stop, the person behind might not be expecting this, which might have disastrous consequences. By the same token, if you go through the crossing at speed, you might just encounter a pedestrian who exercises his right of way and expects oncoming traffic to stop.

Malawian drivers try to be courteous and signal to traffic following them when it is safe to overtake. They do this by operating the left indicator. Conversely, the right indicator is used to let you know that it is dangerous to overtake as oncoming traffic is approaching.

These signals are employed in addition to the conventional uses of indicators and it is up to the driver to discern why they are being used at a particular time.

Maps

A fairly wide range of maps is available from the Department of Map Surveys, which has offices both in Blantyre and Lilongwe (see page 184 for addresses).

Accidents

If an accident takes place and there is injury to any persons involved or damage to property, then the nearest police station must be notified as soon as possible. In accidents where no injury is caused or there is only minor damage to property and if the parties involved are in agreement, then it is sufficient for names and addresses to be exchanged with a view to instituting insurance claims.

After an accident, it is a legal requirement that drivers involved do stop and they and/or their passengers have a right to request names and addresses, vehicle registration number and ownership details, insurance details and particulars of those who might be witnesses.

Should any livestock be killed or injured, then the most you might have to do to placate the owner is to offer payment in compensation for the loss of the animal involved, even if the animal caused the accident. It is futile to expect the owner to have the means to pay for any damage to one's vehicle.

Driving hazards

Whenever possible, avoid driving after dark. Because the majority of roads are unfenced, there is a very high risk of hitting livestock such as cows and goats. At night these present even more of a problem as they sometimes seek out the warmth of the tarmac, particularly in the cooler months.

Other hazards that are likely to be encountered on the roads include pedestrians, cyclists, and vehicles that are parked in dangerous spots.

Be wary at night of vehicles without headlights or indicators. As there are only a handful of traffic lights in the whole of Malawi the chances of encountering drivers from rural areas who may never have come across traffic lights before are extremely high. Consequently, the lights are sometimes ignored.

STANDARD ROUTES

Once you have decided which parts of Malawi you wish to visit, consult this section for ways in which to plan your route. Bear in mind that the quality of roads, particularly those that are untarred, changes with the season. Consequently, the use of a four-wheel-drive vehicle becomes a necessity if you plan to visit some of the more remote areas, particularly during the wet season.

The descriptions of routes and the length of time it takes to get from place to place are subjective and may differ from your perceptions and actual experiences. Please regard these descriptions rather as guides than hard and fast rules.

Distances have been taken from the Ministry of Works and Supplies' Roads Department publication *Road Distance Charts and Maps*, published in November 1986. Copies of this publication are available from the Secretary of Works and Supplies (see page 184 for address).

Route 1: Lilongwe – Kasungu (M1)

Total distance: 127 km   Time: 1 1/2 hours

The M1 to Kasungu is a fully tarred two-lane road in reasonable condition. Kasungu is a small town with a motel, resthouses, shops, a post office and facilities for basic repairs. Fuel is available in the town. From Kasungu it is a short distance to the Kasungu National Park (see Route 2) or Kamuzu Academy (Route 3).

Route 2: Kasungu – Kasungu National Park/Lifupa Camp (D187)

Total distance: 55 km   Time: 1 hour

Leaving Kasungu you rejoin the M1 heading south and a little way after turn right at the signpost for Kasungu National Park. The tarred surface heads up to a dead end and the road should be followed to the left. Visible just beyond the dead end on the hillside is State Lodge, one of the residences belonging to the Life President. As you turn left the road heads through tobacco fields belonging to the tobacco small-holders. Note the barns on the side of the road where the tobacco leaves are cured. The road also passes through several small villages before reaching the park gates. Once inside the park gates, adhere to the speed limit of 40 km/h and remember not to leave your car as there are wild animals around.

Route 3: Kasungu – Kamuzu Academy – Nkhotakota (S54/M10)

Total distance: 127 km   Time: 2 hours

Distance to Kamuzu Academy: 30 km   Time: 40 minutes

Unless it has been recently graded, this untarred road can be a real bone-shaker. However, once you reach Mtunthama village you are confronted with perfectly tarred roads in excellent condition with painted kerbs, road signs and manicured gardens. The contrast between the ruggedness of the bush and this small area where nature has been subdued is startling.

The S54 continues in an easterly direction down the escarpment, joining the M10, which runs through the Nkhotakota Game Reserve to Nkhotakota on the lakeshore and is a longer alternative to taking Routes 11 and 12 from Lilongwe to Nkhotakota.

Route 4: Kasungu – Mzuzu (M1)

Total distance: 240 km   Time: 3 1/2 hours

To reach Mzuzu, take the M1 in a northerly direction from Kasungu. The road is tarred as far as Chikangawa (pronounced Chickengower), the headquarters of the Viphya Pulp and Paper Project. The Viphya Plateau consists of thousands of hectares of pine forest planted over sweeping hills at heights of between 1 500 and 2 000 m above sea-level.

It is a beautiful area and if you have time it might be worth stopping over at the resthouse which is just off the road at Chikangawa (for booking details, see page 159). Springtime is particularly rewarding for the visitor who will see many species of wild flowers lining the road as well as the odd protea bush. Occasionally vervet monkeys and duiker can be seen crossing the road.

Just beyond Chikangawa keep a look-out for the unusual rock formation known as Elephant Rock, which is visible off the right-hand side of the road. If it is a clear day, it is also worth stopping at Kamuzu Viewsite, which is signposted just to the right of the road.

Although the untarred section of the road is generally well maintained, it can present problems at the height of the rainy season.

Route 5: Mzuzu – Nkhata Bay (M12) – Chintheche – Dwangwa – Nkhotakota (S53)

Distances		Times
Mzuzu – Nkhata Bay	47 km	45 mins
Nkhata Bay – Chintheche	49 km	45 mins
Chintheche – Dwangwa	91 km	1 1/2 hours
Dwangwa – Nkhotakota	57 km	45 mins

The road between Mzuzu and Nkhata Bay is tarred and takes you down the escarpment on a scenic drive through pine and rubber plantations. Nkhata Bay (see page 39) is a port for the *Ilala* and *Mtendere*. It also boasts a fine beach, Chikale Beach, just 3 km from the town's centre.

From Nkhata Bay heading in a southerly direction along the coastline, the road is untarred as far as Dwangwa and is likely to present problems during the rains. The tea estates of the Northern Region are visible on the right of the road.

Chintheche is worth a stopover, if only for its beautiful beach. Ten kilometres further south is the New Bandawe mission station (see page 25).

From Chintheche continuing southwards, the road follows the coastline, passing through the villages of Tukombo and Dwambazi, which lies on the border between the Northern and Central Regions. Thirty-nine kilometres south of this border lie the sugar-cane fields of Dwangwa. The Sugar Corporation of Malawi, which owns the estate, has a club which can be reached by turning right off the main road at Dwangwa. Accommodation is available here (see page 159) and it might be worth using the area as a stop-off point for a visit to Nkhotakota Game Reserve which is further south.

The road between Dwangwa and Nkhotakota is tarred but during a particularly heavy rainy season, as occurred in 1989, the road may be damaged as a result of flooding.

Nkhotakota has a resthouse, shopping and refuelling facilities. The *Ilala* anchors offshore and can be reached by lighter if you wish to board her at this point.

Route 6: Mzuzu – Rumphi turnoff (M1)

Total distance: 64 km   Time: 1 hour

The M1 between Mzuzu and Rumphi turnoff is tarred and in fair condition. At the junction between the S85 and D10 you can either head to the left towards Rumphi and Nyika National Park or Vwaza Marsh or take the turning to the right and join the D10, which will lead to the town of Chitimba on the lakeshore via Livingstonia (Route 8).

Route 7: M1/S85 junction – Rumphi (S85) – Chelinda Camp, Nyika National Park (S10)

Total distance: 75 km   Time: up to 2 hours

Join the untarred S85 from the M1 and pass through Rumphi, a small town with a few shops, a resthouse and fuel (it is advisable to fill your fuel tank here, in case fuel is not available in Nyika National Park).

A distance of approximately 40 km separates Rumphi and Thazima Gate at the entrance to the park. Tourists are advised to schedule enough travelling time to reach the gate by 16h00 as it is not advisable to drive through the park after dark.

The climbing, winding road can be impassable to saloon cars during the wet season and it is best to make advance enquiries regarding its condition. Outside the rainy season, the road ranges from being bumpy to very corrugated.

As the road climbs the difference in vegetation types is fairly marked, particularly during springtime when the wildflowers are in bloom, while in autumn the protea bushes on the lower slopes of the plateau are very noticeable. Superb views to Zambia in the west can be enjoyed from different points as the road climbs. Towards the upper reaches of the plateau, the change in topography is dramatic and it is easy to imagine that you have left Africa behind and have arrived in the rolling downland of England or Scotland.

Route 8: Rumphi junction – Livingstonia – Chitimba (S86)

Total distance: 69 km   Time: up to 2 hours

To visit Livingstonia, take the untarred S86 from the M1 and travel for a distance of about 56 km. Again, the road's condition depends on the severity of the previous wet season. During the wet season itself, the use of a four-wheel-drive vehicle is advised. If you want to travel down the escarpment road to Chitimba after Livingstonia, then a four-wheel-drive vehicle is mandatory. The untarred escarpment road with its 20 hairpin bends is likely to be very dangerous during the wet season even for those in four-wheel-drive vehicles, as mud slides can occur and block the road in parts. This section of the road is the width of a single lane only and it may be necessary for larger vehicles to do a type of three-point-turn manoeuvre to get round some of the bends. Allow yourself approximately one hour to do the 15 km. The view from the escarpment road over the lake is spectacular but you might be too busy concentrating on the road to do much sightseeing. This road is not for the fainthearted, nor for vehicles that are likely to break down!

Accommodation is available in the Old Stone House at the Livingstonia Mission (see page 157 for more details), from where you can visit the nearby Manchewe Falls and Khondowe Rock Shelters. If accommodation is fully booked at the Mission, you could try Nchenachena Cottage at Nchenachena, about halfway between Rumphi junction and Livingstonia Mission.

Chitimba, on the lakeshore, is the penultimate port for the *Ilala* and *Mtendere* steamers on their way to the Chilumba Jetty, where they both dock overnight before resuming their return journey southwards.

Route 9: Rumphi turnoff – Chitimba (M1)

Total distance: 71 km   Time: 1 hour

This scenic road is tarred all the way to Chitimba and is a better bet than the untarred S86 which bypasses Livingstonia, if you don't intend to visit the Mission, but rather just want to reach the lakeshore.

However, if you do want to visit the mission, you can still take the M1 and join up with the S86 via the 7 km long D10. This will cut out about 20 km of travel on untarred road.

Route 10: Chitimba – Chilumba jetty – Karonga (M1, S76)

Total distance: 98 km   Time: 1 1/2 hours

The tarred M1 between Chitimba and Karonga passes through lake-shore plains dotted with fat, chunky baobabs and housing the paddy-fields that produce much of Malawi's rice crop.

Chilumba is the final port of call of the *Ilala* and *Mtendere* before they return to the south. Depending on your mode of transport you might consider either catching the bus to Chilumba or driving your hired vehicle there (having made arrangements for it to be collected or having hired a chauffeur so that it can be returned to its depot) and board one of the boats for the journey to the south (see page 125 for more details on the *Ilala's* journey) or you might do the trip in reverse, which entails sailing up from the south.

Karonga is the largest settlement in the far northern reaches of Malawi and it lies on the road to Tanzania, just 49 km south of the border between the two countries. There are basic shopping facilities, fuel and resthouse accommodation in the town.

Route 11: Lilongwe – Livingstonia Beach (via Salima) (M5)

Total distance: 125 km   Time: 1 1/2 hours

The road between Lilongwe and Salima consists of a single-strip tarred surface which is in pretty poor condition. From Salima to Livingstonia Beach Hotel on the lakeshore, however, the road is double width for part of the way and in much better condition.

The section between Lilongwe and Salima can be dangerous, as quite a number of fairly large trucks and buses use it. If you see one of these vehicles approaching, it's best to move off the road and give it as much leeway as you can, for they sometimes travel at speed. As with other roads in Malawi, be on the lookout for pedestrians, cyclists and livestock.

From Lilongwe the road winds along the top of the plateau before it starts wending its way fairly undramatically down the escarpment to the lakeshore plain. The change in the landscape between the most extreme parts of the wet and dry seasons is remarkable, for after the rains have fallen, all is green and lush in a very tropical sort of way, while in the depths of winter, the landscape is clothed in tints of dry, sombre brown.

The road passes through Dowa, a medium-sized village where one can buy a cold drink from one of the bars on the side of the road. Fairly recently, in this district, a man was said to have been killed by a lion while walking home at night after a party.

The road passes quite a number of villages with houses set out in traditional format, as in most other villages in Malawi. The format followed generally has the most important male member of a group owning the largest house, which is set amidst some smaller huts belonging to the female and less important members of a family.

Huts are mostly made out of mud and thatched with long, dried grass, the ends of which are often left untrimmed, giving the impression of an untidy fringe over a little boy's eyes. Keep a lookout for the community's food store and chicken houses. The food store is usually a fairly large, cylindrical container woven out of reeds. It stands on stilts above the ground so that rats and other such thieves cannot easily get at the stores of maize. The chicken house is a much smaller grass structure also standing on stilts, and sometimes linked with the ground by means of a rickety ladder.

From a distance, the clusters of huts are often inconspicuous, particularly in the dry season when the thatched roofs blend in with the dull colours of the surrounding landscape. If you make an effort to look for huts within the landscape, they suddenly become noticeable and the realisation dawns that there are far more huts around than you first imagined. Sometimes it seems that there are always people around, even in the middle of the bush, and in fact Malawi is one of the most densely populated countries in Africa, with a slightly bigger population than Zambia, which is a much larger country.

Salima is a small town with a number of nightclubs and restaurants as well as a basic open-air market and petrol station. From this point, the M17 heads south towards Liwonde and Mangochi (see route 13).

The town and surrounding villages were battered by floods and an earthquake in 1989. During the floods people were seen to be fishing from the side of the road and dugouts were even used as a means of transport. Many of the mud huts, rendered unstable by the floods, collapsed when the earthquake (measuring 6.3 on the Richter scale) struck afterwards.

From Salima, continuing to the lake, the road crosses the swampy lakeshore plain, which houses a rich variety of birdlife and is a favourite haunt of local ornithologists. Just after the marshy area is crossed, a turnoff to the right leads to the Tropical Fish Holding Centre (see page 96), which is worth a visit.

The road ends at the entrance to Livingstonia Beach Hotel (see page 169).

Route 12: Salima – Nkhotakota (M5/S33)

Total distance: 110 km   Time: 1 1/2 hours

The S33 is a tarred, two-lane road in good condition. A few kilometres before Nkhotakota the road crosses over the inlet to Chia Lagoon, an expanse of water that provides a fairly rich source of fish for local fishermen.

Route 13: Salima – Balaka (M17/M1)

Total distance: 139 km   Time: 2 1/2 hours

The tarred M17 is in poor condition although efforts are occasionally made to patch it in places. Possibly the reason why the road has been allowed to deteriorate to such an extent is the fact that a new road is due to be constructed in its place. Drivers should take particular care to avoid potholes on this road.

Chipoka, a major railhead and port for the *Ilala*, is some 27 km from Salima and is reached from the M17 by taking a signposted turnoff to the left. The road runs parallel to the railway line, the existence of which possibly gave the village of Mtakataka its onomatopoeic name.

A few kilometres south of Mtakataka lies the White Fathers' Mission at Mua, worth visiting for a look at its woodcarvings (see page 63).

Soon after the turnoff to Mua on the right, the M18 branches off to the left of the M17 and heads in the direction of the lake (see route 14). Continuing in a southerly direction on the M18 after passing Mua, the road eventually comes out at the M1 slightly north of Balaka township. Given the state of the road, there is not much reason for tourists to use it as a number of far better alternatives are available.

Route 14: Mua – Lakeshore road, south of Monkey Bay (M18)

Total distance: 58 km   Time: 1 hour

This road (M18) is in even worse condition than the M17 described above. This is possibly because it is a black-top road, that is, tar sprayed on gravel only, which accounts for the fact that quite a few sections have been completely washed away.

As it passes a fairly low-lying section of the lakeshore plain, there are a few drifts to be crossed that might become impassable during the rainy season.

Parts of the lake are visible on the left, and the scenery is pleasantly tropical. Keep a lookout for smallholder cotton plantations.

A fair collection of curios are on sale at the end of the M18 where it meets with the Monkey Bay/Mangochi Road. Prices here are likely to be much lower than those nearer the lakeshore hotels or in the cities. At the junction, you can either turn left for Monkey Bay and Cape Maclear or right for Club Makokola, Nkopola Lodge, Palm Beach and Mangochi.

Route 15: Junction of M18 with Monkey Bay/Mangochi Road – Monkey Bay (M15)

Total distance: 12 km   Time: 10 minutes

Heading northwards from the point where the M18 meets the Monkey Bay/Mangochi Road (M15), the road continues for a distance of 12 km before ending at the entrance to the harbour at Monkey Bay. On this same road, after a distance of about 6 km, there is a turnoff to the left signposted "Lake Malawi National Park" and "Golden Sands". This mostly untarred road winds through really scenic countryside bordered by rocky hills encrusted with huge boulders. The road is in reasonable condition but may present problems during the height of the wet season. Fortunately, over the steeper sections of the route the road is tarred.

Just a few kilometres past this section you will notice a signpost pointing to a path leading off to the right of the road. This indicates the site of Mwalamphini, the rock of tribal markings. The scratches on the rock have apparently been created by natural forces.

Soon after the lake becomes visible in the distance there are two unmarked turnoffs to the right. These both lead to Chembe village, a fairly large fishing village on the shores of the lake facing Thumbi Island West and Domwe Island. To reach Stevens' Resthouse take the second turnoff, which heads into the village, and then turn left once you have reached the middle of the village. The actual roadway isn't very clear but if you get lost just ask a villager the way to the resthouse, which is not more than a few hundred metres away.

To reach Golden Sands Holiday Camp (see page 169 for details) continue past these turnoffs for about another 2 km. At this point there is an entrance gate to the Lake Malawi National Park area where entry fees are payable by all those who wish to enter the park and Cape Maclear area.

Route 16: Junction of M18 with Monkey Bay/Mangochi Road – Mangochi (M15)

Total distance: 50 km   Time: approximately 45 minutes

This is the same road as that described above (M15), heading in a southerly direction towards Mangochi. The tarred road is in excellent condition and runs through the lakeshore plain, which is dotted with baobabs, borassus palms, mango and banana trees and the occasional "sausage" tree, with its large sausage-like fruit.

The road runs past the turnoffs to Club Makokola and Nkopola Lodge and Leisure Centre, which are within about 5 km of each other. A few kilometres thereafter, on the left, are the turnoffs to Maldeco Fisheries and the Palm Beach Holiday Resort.

Route 17: Mangochi – M1 junction near Liwonde (M3)

Total distance: 69 km   Time: just under an hour

The tarred M17, which is in excellent condition, is the continuation of Route 16 described above.

One passes through the typical lakeshore plain scenery of baobabs, mango trees and palms, through fishing villages which have thousands of tiny silver fish glinting in the sunlight as they dry on makeshift racks on the side of the road.

This section of road is particularly noted for the large circular grass mats displayed for sale on the side of the road. There are many pedestrians about and it is wise to keep a watchful eye out for them and the clumps of goats and cows who seem to enjoy standing motionless in the middle of the road.

Dotted along the side of the road are several vendors selling fresh and dried coconuts as well as mangoes, tomatoes, pumpkins, citrus fruit and bananas, depending on the season. You'll also see a number of mosques tucked away off the road, the modern embodiments of the religious legacy of the Arab slave traders just over a century ago.

A few kilometres past Mangochi, to the left of the road you'll catch sight of Lake Malombe (see page 28).

At the end of the road, where it joins with the Blantyre/Lilongwe M1, stands an assortment of stalls where a variety of curios and chairs may be purchased.

Route 18: Lilongwe – Blantyre (M1/M2)

Total distance: 312 km   Time: 3 1/2 to 4 hours

The entire road is tarred with two lanes, as befits a road linking the country's two largest and most important cities. The 119 km stretch of road from a point just 8 km north of Balaka all the way to Blantyre was constructed in 1989 and so is in tip-top condition.

A distance of 83 km separates Lilongwe from Dedza, a sizeable town situated in a fairly mountainous region. This is immediately apparent by the cooler temperatures and mists that are often experienced in the area. Just 18 km before Dedza is a turnoff to the Chencherere Rock Shelters in the Chongoni Forest Reserve, where Bushman-type paintings might be of interest.

Tourists might like to pay a visit to the Dedza Potteries in the town, taking the first entrance to the town to be reached from the Lilongwe side. The pottery's exact location is indicated by signposts about 2 km from the main road.

Just before leaving the Dedza area, the motorist will pass through a police roadblock. You may be required to show your passport and to have your boot searched. From this point onwards to Ntcheu, the road forms the border between Malawi and Mozambique for a distance of 75 km. Obviously the police are wary of incursions from the Mozambique side and like to keep tabs on traffic between the two main centres.

Scenery along this road is very pleasant and varied, according to the season. Between Dedza and Ntcheu there are a number of points from where distant views across the lake can be enjoyed.

Before the new section of road was constructed, the M1 continued south through Balaka, Liwonde and Zomba to Blantyre.

Route 19: Balaka (via Liwonde) – Zomba (M1)

Total distance: 65 km   Time: approximately 45 minutes

This route is a continuation of the M1 as described in Route 18 and it served as the main road from Lilongwe to Blantyre until the M2 was opened in 1989. It is slightly longer (about 40 km) but a visit to Zomba certainly makes up for the extra journey if you are not in a rush.

Between Balaka and the Kamuzu Barrage on the Shire River (31 km) the road drops slightly and without too much variation in scenery. You'll pass the turnoff to the lake about 28 km south of Balaka. If you want to peruse the wares of the curio sellers, this is a good place to stop. Prices are reasonable here and you might find one or two unusual items. If you need to stop for a drink try the Manpower Restaurant just a few hundred metres up the lake road from the junction.

From this junction, continuing to Zomba, you will pass a village just before entering the Kamuzu Barrage. There is a small market on the side of the road and fish can be purchased here. More often than not there is a police check. The road to Kudya Discovery Lodge is to the left through the village.

About a kilometre past the Barrage is the turnoff to the township of Liwonde and the road leading to the Liwonde National Park. Continuing along the M1, the road begins to climb as it leaves the valley floor. You'll notice pockets of makeshift kiosks on the side of the road, where the "chief's chairs" are lined up for display. This area has the widest selection of designs for these chairs and prices are reasonable too.

The road gets steeper as it ascends the foothills of the Shire Highlands and to the right, just as the road begins to level out, you will notice a splendid view into the distance across the Shire Valley. Just after Machinga village, in a dip on the left-hand side of the road, are some palmwood chairs and tables lined up on display (see page 90 for description of palmwood).

Past this area the road skirts round the eastern foothills of Zomba Plateau before making its entrance to the town. Lake Chilwa is sometimes visible in the distance to the left of the road.

Route 20: Zomba – Blantyre (M1)

Total distance: 69 km   Time: just under an hour

This route was recently rehabilitated and is now quite serviceable. It passes along the spine of the Shire Highlands. Far in the distance to the left you might catch sight of Mulanje if visibility is clear.

An assortment of villages cluster together here and there along the side of the road, some with quaintly named bars, restaurants and tea-rooms. On the right-hand side of the road just past midway, you might see a variety of clay pots displayed for sale. Apart from Lilongwe market, this is one of the best places to stop for pottery. Fruit and vegetables in season are also sold at this point.

As the road approaches Blantyre, more and more settlements line the sides of the road. Also visible are the coffee trees of farming estates. The road enters the city through the suburb of Limbe.

Route 21: Blantyre – Thyolo – Mulanje (M1)

Total distance: 88 km	Time: 90 minutes
Distance to Thyolo: 41 km	Time: 45 minutes
Distance Thyolo to Mulanje: 47 km	Time: 45 minutes

The road to Thyolo (pronounced Cholo) and Mulanje is a continuation of the M1. However, as it leaves the outskirts of Limbe it changes from a two-lane into a single-lane road. Watch out for signs to Bvumbwe Agricultural Research Station and Gangecraft curio workshop (see page 90) on the right. Caution is needed on this road especially during mist and rain or towards sunset and after dark.

Despite the condition of the road it is a most pleasant experience to drive through the tea plantations that cover the rolling hills to the sides of the road, and particularly rewarding during the dry season when the drab vegetation of the surrounding countryside is vividly contrasted by the refreshing emerald green of the tea bushes. During the height of the tea-picking season, from September to December, you'll notice teams of tea-pickers at work in the plantations. Each picker is allotted a section of his own to cover and as he picks the leaves he drops them into a basket on his back.

Keep a look-out when driving along this road for a viewpoint on the left of the road. It is worth stopping here and admiring the grandeur of Mulanje Massif in the distance.

Before you reach the town of Thyolo, you will see two turnoffs to the right leading to the Thyolo Club. If you have time try stopping at the club to enjoy a marvellous cup of Thyolo tea. From Thyolo (which is just halfway between Blantyre and Mulanje) the road descends to the Phalombe Plain and the tea estates begin to thin out, giving way to maize and other plantations.

After you cross the railway line at Luchenza you may be interested in stopping off in the village to visit the Luchenza Pottery, located in one of the small ageing buildings on the left of the road. As it is unmarked, just ask a passer-by to show you the shop. The range of items available is not large but there might just be something to catch your fancy.

A distance of 27 km separates Luchenza from Mulanje.

Route 22: Blantyre – Chikwawa – Nsanje (S38)

Total distance: 173 km	Time: approximately 3 hours
Distance to Chikwawa 54 km	Time: 40 minutes
Distance to Nchalo 79 km	Time: at least 1 hour

To reach the Chikwawa road drive along Victoria Avenue and pass the Blantyre Club entrance on your right, cross over the small bridge and take the second turning right, which is signposted. The road runs past a number of villages in a fairly undramatic way before it begins its 16 km long, steep 900 m descent to the floor of the lower Shire Valley. A word of warning: at the height of the rains, extra caution is advised as mudslides can occur, as evidenced by a huge boulder that seems to have slipped onto the shoulder of the road.

On a clear day there are magnificent views while you negotiate the several hairpin bends along this route. In the distance lies the silver ribbon of the Shire River as it lazily unwinds on its descent to the Zambezi River and ultimately the Indian Ocean. If you look carefully you can pick out the sugar-cane fields of the Sucoma sugar plantations at Nchalo.

Once the road reaches the valley floor, which at some points, is not more than 37 m above sea-level, it crosses the floodplain to the Kamuzu Bridge spanning the Shire. There is usually a police check at the end of the bridge. About 100 or 200 metres past the check is the signposted turnoff for Chikwawa, Majete Game Reserve and Kapichira Falls.

Continuing towards Nchalo the road is in poor condition and can be difficult to negotiate during the rains when there is plenty of mud about.

This area was severely damaged by floods during the 1989 rainy season and many people were left homeless. There are two entrances to Lengwe National Park. It is recommended that you take the second, which is about 20 km from the checkpoint at the bridge. At Nchalo, 11 km past this second entrance, you will see the entrance to Sucoma, where chalet accommodation may be available (see page 167). Even if you do not plan to stay at Sucoma you might enjoy a visit to the clubhouse on the banks of the Shire, where depending on the weather, you can swim in the pool or down a cold "Green" while you watch the fast-flowing river. It may also be possible to persuade the boatman to take you for a ride on his "African Queen" type launch.

At Nchalo itself there is a well-stocked supermarket, a resthouse or two and a petrol station.

The S38 continues through Nchalo heading in a southerly direction for Ngabu, Bangula, Nsanje and the most southerly tip of Malawi. Areas of interest that are accessible from this road are the Elephant Marsh to the east and Mwabvi Game Reserve to the west. However, the road has been severely damaged by flooding in recent years and its condition is more suited to four-wheel-drive vehicles.

AIR TRANSPORT

Daily flights between Lilongwe and Blantyre are made by the national carrier, Air Malawi. There are also three flights a week from Lilongwe to Mzuzu and Karonga in the Northern Region. There are plans to put a private service into operation, linking Club Makokola and Kamuzu International Airport. Club Makokola, which has its own airstrip, also arranges charter flights for tourists.

A company called Air Charters Limited operates charter flights from Chileka Airport in Blantyre (see address details on page 184). The company has four planes ranging in size from a three-seater to an eight-seater. Flights can be arranged to Club Makokola, Zomba, Salima, Kasungu National Park, Nyika National Park, Likoma Island, Lilongwe, Mzuzu and Karonga.

BOAT TRANSPORT

The sheer size and navigability of Lake Malawi and its outlet, the Shire River, make it ideal for exploration purposes by boats both large and small.

The m.v. (motor vessel) *Ilala* and m.v. *Mtendere* are the major commercial and passenger carriers on the lake, while smaller vessels such as the *Sunbird* and *Shire Princess* are purely pleasure craft whose facilities are aimed at the tourist industry.

A trip on the *Ilala*

A trip on Malawi's mini-liner from the southerly tip of Lake Malawi to near its most northerly extremity is still one of those undiscovered delights, a rare adventure of a different kind which, once experienced, is likely to be forever remembered and cherished as something special.

Built in 1951, the *Ilala*, a 620 ton twin-screw vessel which carries ten cabin-class passengers and 350 lower-deck passengers, has undertaken the same trip for 11 months of the year, week in and week out for more than 35 years.

The *Ilala I*, the first steamer to sail the lake, was launched in 1875. Named after the place in Zambia where David Livingstone died, it was brought out from Britain by the early members of the Livingstonia Mission of the Free Church of Scotland, and afterwards taken over by the African Lakes Company in 1882. The boat, which was much smaller than the present *Ilala*, is believed to have sunk in about 1922.

Joining the *Ilala* for her full round trip is an ideal way of seeing parts of the lake that would be inaccessible by car. One may also choose to combine a three, five or six day trip on the boat with a week spent in the national parks and/or a week spent at a resort on the lakeshore.

Once a year, the boat is taken into dry dock for refitting purposes. Of course, if it is in need of urgent repairs at any other time it will again be taken out of commission. This may present the tourist with a problem, for, if a berth in cabin class is booked (which must be done at least two months in advance), there is a fair risk that the tourist will arrive in Malawi only to find that his trip has been cancelled. It's something to be forewarned about and make provision for so that disappointment can be avoided.

Far from being a luxury cruiser with champagne on tap, the *Ilala* is primarily a cargo boat, fetching and carrying cargo of all types to and from remote parts of the lake that would be inaccessible by land in some instances. It also acts as a bus service, ferrying people from one tiny port to another, or as an intermediate means of transport from village to capital city.

You will see goats and chickens and baskets of ripe red tomatoes, mangoes, oranges, bananas, peanuts, stinky dried fish, bicycles, sewing machines and anything else that can conceivably be carried.

The lowest of the three decks is reserved for third-class passengers who pay a minimal fare for rudimentary seating accommodation, and often only standing accommodation. Second-class passengers are on the same level but have a slightly more sophisticated and sheltered seating arrangement.

Oliver Ransford, in his outstanding historical account of Malawi, *Livingstone's Lake*, describes the atmosphere on board so well that it must be quoted: "Each day on board, amid the excited bell ringing, siren shrieks and hooting that seem inseparable from all maritime arrivals and departures, laughing crowds of Malawians line up on the *Ilala*'s deck to disembark, cluttered up with baggage that includes bicycles, cages filled with squawking fowls, sewing machines and even tethered goats. They are ferried ashore in lighters to return an hour or so later crammed with another batch of passengers who quickly settle down in their cramped quarters to cards and singing and sleeping and the preparation of meals in little cooking pots. It all looks and sounds like a cross between Hampstead Heath on a Bank holiday and an Eastern market, but when the ship weighs anchor again the noise dies down and the first-class passengers . . . resume their novels, their deck chairs and their worship of the sun."

Only 12 first-class passengers can be accommodated on the boat in four double and two single cabins on the middle deck. Each cabin has two single beds, a dressing table with mirror and stool, a cupboard with hanging space and a washbasin.

Separate toilets outside the cabins are reserved for the exclusive use of ladies or gentlemen travelling in first class, but their condition suggests that they are more widely used. A communal bath and shower is also available, but it is suggested that a "basin bath" is taken in the privacy and relative cleanliness of your cabin instead.

You can reserve the "owner's cabin", which has its own shower and toilet, so if you prefer this option, book well in advance to be sure of securing this particular cabin.

The middle deck also houses the dining room, lounge and galley as well as staff quarters and the upper deck is where the first-class tourists spend most of their time when not sleeping or eating. Second- and third-class passengers are denied access to the middle and upper decks, which are reserved for the exclusive use of the first-class passengers.

The upper deck is open to the elements except for a well-stocked bar area which offers some shelter from the sun and the wind. There's nothing much else to do during the daylight hours except to spend your time on the top deck, either sunning yourself in a deckchair out in the open or sheltered beneath the shade of the bar's roof. Either way there is much to be said for just lazily watching the magnificent scenery at the edge of the lake go by at a gentle 10 knots.

In Malawi there is no better way to get away from it all and still get to see and appreciate the country without expending much effort. However, be warned that if you insist on five-star luxury, you might be somewhat disillusioned. Only the more tolerant and possibly adventurous type of traveller is likely to enjoy the *Ilala* trip. You would do well not to drink the water on board unless it has been boiled. All tap water is said to come from the lake and it is difficult to judge how clean it is.

It is said that the wise tourist will take his trip between March and September, these being the cooler months. Thereafter as the rainy season approaches and storms and squalls become more common, there is a greater risk of developing sea-sickness. October and November are also likely to be extremely hot months which may cause some discomfort while the months from March to May are likely to be the calmest but not necessarily the coolest.

Every Friday morning the boat leaves from its home port in Monkey Bay in the south. Be prepared for a delay of up to six hours in some cases. If the boat is late, then the captain will cut down time spent at ports and even visits to certain less important ports in an attempt to make up for lost time.

The boat crosses the lake from Monkey Bay to Makanjila, a settlement in the most northerly sector of Malawi on the eastern side of the lake. Then it heads back across the lake to Chipoka on its westerly shore. There is usually a fairly long stop at Chipoka as it is the nearest stop to Lilongwe and therefore an important cargo loading point (see route section, page 117). You could choose to join the boat here after driving from Lilongwe.

From Chipoka the boat heads for Nkhotakota, which it reaches at dawn. If the boat is a bit late, you might experience the happy coincidence of a magnificent sunrise over the lake with the early morning tea call and arrival at Nkhotakota.

The boat docks out at sea in order to avoid the winding sandbanks that give Nkhotakota its name, but a motorised lifeboat goes ashore to drop off and collect passengers. Nkhotakota is not very visible from the boat but for an hour long stop, it is not really worth disembarking.

The *Ilala* then weighs anchor and heads off once again across the lake to Likoma and its sister island, Chizumulu. These are Malawian territory in Mozambican waters, lying off a seemingly uninhabited stretch of Mozambique which can clearly be seen from the boat.

Likoma, the lake's largest island, was at one stage said to be the only place in Africa with a 100 per cent literacy rate, something which has been attributed to the zealous work of the missionaries who lived on the island (see page 59). The trip to the island takes a steady six and a half hours with not much to see except a slowly disappearing Malawian shore from one side of the boat and a slowly appearing Mozambican shore on the other side.

It's best to enjoy a three-course breakfast and then sleep it off on the top deck in the early morning sun. Be extremely careful about your exposure to the sunlight reflected off the water, which can inflict far greater burns than would occur ashore. If the weather is sunny, you can suntan as you sit under the canopy that houses the bar.

The *Ilala* anchors offshore at Likoma Island (see page 59), which seems surprisingly large from the water and rather barren compared with the lakeshore vegetation seen elsewhere. This is apparently due to the fact that Likoma lies in the rainshadow of the Mozambican shore.

At Likoma it is worth fighting for a place on one of the lifeboats to get ashore as the boat stops for an hour and in that time it is possible to manage a quick tour of the most important part of the island and those parts most accessible from the boat. The landing stage is on a small beach set amidst some bars and tiny shops and the walk up through the neatly arranged houses to Likoma's main attraction, its cathedral, is clearly visible.

The imposing building known as St Peter's Anglican Cathedral was built by members of the Universities Mission to Central Africa in the first decade of this century. Matching Winchester Cathedral in size, the building had been allowed to deteriorate badly prior to 1970 when the Life President visited the island and started a fund for the restoration of the cathedral to its former glory. Work on the project was completed in 1986, in time for the centenary of the establishment of the Anglican mission on the island.

Some tourists choose to leave the *Ilala* at this point and stay on the island, either camping or at the government resthouse. The *Ilala*'s schedule requires that the visitor remains on Likoma for Saturday, Sunday and Monday nights and embarks again for the boat's southward bound journey when it calls back early on Tuesday morning.

If your schedule is tight it may be possible to book your trip in such a way that you sail to the island on the *Ilala*, arriving on Saturday at midday and, after spending the night there, leave Likoma early the next morning on the *Mtendere* for more southerly ports.

There's not much to do except swim, explore the island and get to know the locals and if you have time to kill and are equipped with adequate provisions, then a stay might be a worthwhile proposition (see page 159).

From Likoma the boat heads for the neighbouring but smaller Chizimulu Island, which is an hour and a half away. After an hour's stop it leaves again for Nkhata Bay, once more across the lake on the westerly shore, the trip taking approximately three and a half hours. The *Ilala* lies in port at Nkhata Bay for most of the night and leaves again early on Sunday morning.

Although the top deck is spacious and reserved for the relaxation of the first-class passengers this rule is waived when the boat visits certain ports. The top deck then becomes open to visitors from ashore and evidently represents a highlight in their lives as a weekly opportunity to dress up and bring their family and friends aboard for a drink, which is, more often than not, non-alcoholic. As with anywhere else in Malawi you are likely to meet polite, pleasant people many of whom seem to be very keen to correspond. Before you know it you will have a list of addresses of instant penpals! You may also get friendly requests to take a photograph or two of these budding correspondents.

Nkhata Bay (see page 39) is a pleasant little port which is well worth wandering around on the southward-bound trip when the boat docks earlier in the afternoon. It is backed by the foothills of the Viphya Plateau, where Livingstone and his party got lost and nearly died.

Nkhata Bay is also the site of the first major uprising of the Malawian people against white rule. Forty martyrs to this cause died here in 1959, an event which is commemorated every year on 3 March as Martyr's Day.

The first port of call in the morning is Usisya. From this point onwards, the shoreline begins to rise up steeply from the lake. It is a prelude to the magnificent scenery which, as you continue northwards, consists more and more of the forbidding barrier formed by the steeply angled walls of the Rift Valley as it narrows. In keeping with this change in the landscape, the lake's waters are at their deepest in this region. Because most of the edible fish are caught in shallower waters, there is less of a harvest here than there is in the more southerly portions of the lake.

From this point onwards the scenery is truly spectacular. Here and there you will notice that quite a number of the few houses dotting the landscape are built of more sophisticated materials. You might wonder how these materials were transported to such isolated spots. Apparently the houses belong to men who went to work on the South African gold mines. Having made their fortunes they brought back their money and invested it in good quality building materials that were then transported by boat to their chosen sites.

Ruarwe, another charming lakeside village on the *Ilala's* itinerary, lies an hour's journey from Usisya.

With short hauls lasting no more than an hour and stops of up to an hour in duration, there's always something interesting to watch.

While the boat is anchored you will never tire of watching the disembarking passengers, some dressed in three-piece suits, hurriedly offload their *katundu* (baggage) onto the noisy lighter that will take them ashore while the ever-present lake merchants in their dugout canoes, keen not to miss the possibility of a sale in these more remote parts, busily ply their trade of fresh fruit or vegetables or even fish to peckish passengers remaining on the boat.

The villages of Usisya, Ruarwe and Mlowe have that special quality about them of time seeming to have stood still. Life here seems to be ruled by the necessity for survival only. The people here live in paradise: they have the lake, their food and sport and they have the sun. The rat race doesn't stand a chance here.

From Ruarwe, the boat continues to Mlowe, then Chitipa and finally Chilumba, hugging the coastline. There is not much to see in Chilumba, the *Ilala's* final port of call on its northward-bound journey, but you could consider going ashore by stepping straight onto the jetty and taking a walk down the high street. If you choose to leave the boat at this point, you could spend the night in the village's basic resthouse before catching the next bus to Nkhata Bay, where you could rejoin the boat the following afternoon.

Very early the next morning the boat leaves Chilumba and begins its southward-bound journey back to the home port, visiting the same ports as it did on the northward-bound journey.

The *Ilala* reaches Monkey Bay at 17h30 on Wednesday afternoon and spends the whole of Thursday in dock until it begins its northward-bound trip on Friday morning again.

The *Mtendere* is another lake bus and follows the same route as the *Ilala*, the main differences between the two being that the *Mtendere* docks on Monday and leaves again on Tuesday and not all the same ports are visited. Cabin-class accommodation and meals are not available on the *Mtendere*, neither does the boat have any facilities for carrying vehicles, as does the *Ilala*. However, the same glorious spectacles await the traveller who is keen to soak in nature at her best while marvelling at the never-ending diversity of human beings.

The following timetable will give the prospective passenger an idea of the boat's movements.

Schedule m.v. *Ilala* with effect from April 1988 (subject to change)

Northbound journey				Southbound journey			
	Arrive		*Depart*		*Arrive*		*Depart*
Monkey Bay	–	Fri	0800	Chilumba	–	Mon	0400
Chilinda	1000		1030	Chitimba	0530		0630
Makanjila	1230		1400	Mlowe	0730		0830
Chipoka	1700	Sat	2130	Ruarwe	1030		1130
Nkhotakota	0500		0600	Usisya	1230		1330
Likoma Is.	1230		1330	Nkhata Bay	1600	Tue	0300
Chizumulu Is.	1500		1600	Chizumulu Is.	0630		0730
Nkhata Bay	1930	Sun	0400	Likoma Is.	0830		1000
Usisya	0630		0730	Nkhotakota	1600		1700
Ruarwe	0830		0930	Chipoka	0200	Wed	0800
Mlowe	1130		1230	Makanjila	1100		1200
Chitimba	1330		1430	Chilinda	1400		1500
Chilumba	1600		–	Monkey Bay	1730		–

Schedule m.v. *Mtendere* with effect from April 1988 (subject to change)

Northbound journey				Southbound journey			
	Arrive		*Depart*		*Arrive*		*Depart*
Monkey Bay	–	Tue	1000	Chilumba	–	Sat	0600
Chipoka	1230		2230	Mlowe	0800		0830
Nkhotakota	0530	Wed	0630	Charo	1000		1100
Likoma Is.	1200		1300	Ruarwe	1200		1300
Chizumulu Is.	1400		1430	Usisya	1330		1430
Nkhata Bay	1730	Thu	0600	Mangwirna Bay	1530		1630
Mangwirna Bay	0700		0730	Nkhata Bay	1730	Sun	0230

Northbound journey				Southbound journey			
	Arrive		*Depart*		*Arrive*		*Depart*
Usisya	0900	Thu	0930	Chizumulu Is.	0530	Sun	0600
Ruarwe	1030		1100	Likoma Is.	0700		0800
Charo	1130		1200	Nkhotakota	1330		1430
Mlowe	1330		1430	Chipoka	2130	Mon	0630
Chilumba	1630	Fri	0600	Monkey Bay	0930		–
Kambwe	0930		1030				
Kaporo	1130		1230				
Chilumba	1700		–				

Detailed fare schedules for both boats are available on application to Malawi Railways Limited (see page 184 for address).

Bookings for cabin-class should be made at least two months in advance. They may be done in writing or by phoning Malawi Railways Limited. In the case of the *Ilala*, you should do your best to see that these bookings are confirmed closer to the intended date of sailing.

Only one car at a time may be put on board the *Ilala* from Chipoka to Nkhata Bay or from Chipoka to Chilumba. The rates vary according to the model and the weight of the car.

For reasons of safety, it is not advisable for children under the age of six to sail on the boats as they might fall through gaps in the boats' railings if they are not under constant supervision. For children over that age it is advisable to bring supplies of games or toys that might help prevent boredom.

The *Sunbird*

Based at Club Makokola, the 40 ton *Sunbird* is much smaller than either the *Ilala* or *Mtendere*, and is geared towards pleasure cruises.

Sundowner cruises to nearby Bird Island (Boadzulu Island) and along the coast are offered and the luxury cruiser, which carries 24 passengers and can accommodate 16 passengers overnight, is also available for special charter.

A particularly enjoyable trip on the *Sunbird* is that from Club Makokola through Lake Malombe and along the Shire River, which borders the Liwonde National Park, to Kudya Discovery Lodge.

The *Shire Princess*

This boat is a pleasure cruiser, based at Kudya Discovery Lodge, on the banks of the Shire River near Liwonde. Cruises lasting three hours usually take place at the weekend although special arrangements can be made for weekly cruises.

The cruise along the Shire River offers the visitor a superb vantage point to observe wildlife from the Liwonde National Park, which tends to congregate at the river. It is likely to be the most rewarding during the dry season when water supplies further within the park are at low levels and the animals are forced to visit the river for their water supply. During the wet season the vegetation is likely to be dense which may inhibit game viewing.

Sailing safaris

Rift Lake Charters, a company based at Club Makokola, offers a range of sailing safaris to suit all tastes. The company's sturdy catamarans can take groups of eight on sundowner cruises to nearby Boadzulu Island as well as for two and three day trips to Cape Maclear that also involve camping and snorkelling.

The company also offers launch trips along the Shire River, bordering the Liwonde National Park. Overnight accommodation is arranged at the Mvuu rest camp on the riverbank. Hiking trips into the park can be catered for.

At the time of writing, Rift Lake Charters was planning to implement a scuba diving training scheme for visitors (see page 184 for address details).

6 FACTORS AFFECTING YOUR PLANNING

A number of factors should be taken into account when planning your trip to Malawi: the seasons and climate, provisions to be made about healthcare and safety, and what items should be brought with you from your country of origin.

SEASONS AND CLIMATE

Taken together, proximity to the lake and altitude variation (from 37 m to 3 002 m above sea-level) are the factors that mostly influence rainfall and temperature.

Places with the coolest mean annual temperatures (i.e. under 20°C) are those above 900 m in altitude: Nyika Plateau and the Viphya in the north, Dedza in the Central Region and Mulanje and the Shire Highlands in the Southern Region. In contrast, the lowest parts of Malawi – the lower Shire Valley in the Southern Region – experience scorching mean maximum temperatures of 37°C.

The seasons in Malawi are clear-cut: the rainy season generally lasts from December to April, and the dry season from May to November. The dry season can be subdivided into the cool dry season, comprising June, July and August, with temperatures rarely falling to freezing at night (except for Nyika and Mulanje) and averaging 18–25°C during the day; and the hot dry season, which falls between September and December, with temperatures climbing to highs of 35°C on some days but averaging about 26–28°C.

Once the rains begin the widespread presence of cloud shields the earth from the sun's baking rays and temperatures drop to a very pleasant average of 22–26°C.

The wet season is really wet and not much fun for the average sun-seeking tourist, whose best chance of finding the sun is at the lakeshore rather than inland.

To compound matters, the rains certainly damage both the tarred and untarred roads, making travel in a two-wheel-drive vehicle a rather limited proposition. Certain national parks are closed for this reason, and tall, dense vegetation at this time of year further inhibits game viewing.

The hot dry season can be really uncomfortable for those who dislike heat. The use of an airconditioning unit or fan can offer much relief. In addition, the sun's rays, being more directly overhead at this time of year, can burn sensitive skin fiercely, making the use of a sun-block preparation mandatory.

Although Malawi's climate makes a visit to the country a year-round proposition in broad terms, the best time to visit is between the cooler dry months of May and September. Many people consider the pivotal seasons of autumn and spring to be the times when Malawi is at her best.

During autumn, the countryside is still swathed in a cloth of vivid green, the sun shines without burning or causing discomfort, swimming in the lake's warm waters is still very pleasant and the roads are starting to dry out, making travel that much easier.

Spring, on the other hand, is the start of a new season of growth, the vegetation loses its sombre tones and hints of new, tender green foliage start appearing, the days are warm and the nights still have a cool piquancy about them, and game viewing is at its most rewarding.

The winter months of June, July and August are the coolest although weather during these months bears no resemblance to the icy coldness of the European winter. In fact, it's not very easy to find the excuse to make an indoor fire except on the Nyika Plateau or on Mulanje, where the need for a fire is greater during a far larger portion of the year. At the lake it's quite possible at this time of year to don a swimsuit, to bask in the sun and even frolic in the water.

The following chart gives an idea of mean minimum and maximum temperatures at the lake throughout the year. It should be stressed that these are average temperatures which do not reflect any extremes that may occur.

Mangochi

	Jan	Feb	Mar	Apr	May	Jun	Jul	Aug	Sep	Oct	Nov	Dec
°C	26	26	25	24	23	20	20	22	24	27	28	27
°F	79	79	77	75	73	68	68	72	75	81	82	81

Water temperatures at the lake

	Jan	Feb	Mar	Apr	May	Jun	Jul	Aug	Sep	Oct	Nov	Dec
°C	28	28	28	27	26	25	24	24	25	27	28	28

The following average maximum and minimum Centigrade tempera-
tures are experienced at Chelinda camp at Nyika National Park in the
Northern Region; Lilongwe in the Central Region; and Blantyre in the
South.

	Maximum	Months	Minimum	Months
Chelinda	22	Oct/Nov	4	July
Lilongwe	33	Oct/Dec	8	July/August
Blantyre	28	Oct/Dec	14	June/July

Best times to visit the parks and reserves

Broadly speaking, it is always best to visit the parks and reserves during
the second half of the dry season. At this time of year water resources
are becoming scarce and game is forced to congregate at the remaining
water-holes. The grass is dry and in many cases has been burnt or eaten
and trampled and visibility is far superior to the wet season when the
thicket is much taller and more dense. Most of the roads have been
repaired during the dry season and access is clear to all the national
parks and reserves.

HEALTH PRECAUTIONS

Malawi's medical facilities can accommodate the majority of illnesses
and emergencies, but cases that require very specialised treatment are
usually referred to South Africa and the United Kingdom.

The two largest cities, Lilongwe and Blantyre, both have large general
hospitals and several general medical and dental practitioners in business (see page 185 for telephone numbers). If an emergency occurs in
the rural areas, it is worth approaching the nearest clinic or dispensary
for immediate assistance.

Visitors who are undergoing treatment for any disorders are advised
to take adequate supplies of any specialised drugs that may be required.

Apart from any other conditions, those that are most particular to
this part of Africa are worth mentioning so that the tourist can be
adequately forewarned and fore-armed before his visit.

It must be stressed that what follows is not intended to frighten off the potential tourist. The chances are that your visit will be trouble-free in health terms. Rather, this section is intended to provide a handy reference for those who may need it, particularly those travellers who aim to travel along less well-trodden paths.

Malaria

Transmitted by mosquitoes, this disease is rife in Malawi, particularly during the wet season as mosquitoes breed in damp locations.

Symptoms

Sometimes symptoms are non-specific but they may include a splitting headache, nausea, flu-like symptoms such as aching joints, fever, tired-ness, and an inability to tolerate bright light. As the disease progresses, feverish sweats are followed by uncontrollable shivering and chills. Diarrhoea and vomiting can be accompanying symptoms.

In certain cases, continued prophylaxis can mask the symptoms until the traveller discontinues prophylaxis, which may be some weeks later when he has returned home. In such circumstances, it is easy to over-look the possibility of the presence of malaria and misdiagnose the condition. Left untreated, malaria can quickly lead to death, therefore if there is any suspicion at all that malaria might be the cause of illness, a course of treatment should be taken immediately.

It is worth knowing that continued prophylaxis can mask the presence of malarial parasites in any blood samples that are analysed.

Protection/prevention

The best form of protection against malaria is the use of prophylactics, a course of which should be commenced at least two weeks before you intend to visit Malawi.

Thereafter they should be taken at the same time on the same day of each week if you are following a weekly regimen, or at the same time every day if you are taking a daily regimen. After leaving the country you should continue to take the prophylactics for at least four weeks, but preferably six to eight weeks.

Medical authorities advise that the use of prophylaxis in pregnancy causes less risk to the foetus than would be caused by contracting the disease itself. However, if you are pregnant, you should possibly think twice about travelling to Malawi.

Chloroquin-resistant strains of the malarial parasite exist in Malawi, consequently you should ask your pharmacist to recommend a prophylactic which does not contain chloroquin. To guard against any temporary shortages of prophylactic drugs in the country, as well as against possible loss of or damage to your supply of tablets, you should always carry a duplicate supply (in a separate place) of the full requirement of tablets needed for your stay in Malawi.

Despite judicious prophylaxis, malaria can still be contracted, but the severity of the disease will be minimised and the risk of death reduced. The use of repellent sprays and creams applied at least twice daily can help you guard against being bitten, especially if you are camping outdoors, when it would be wise to use a mosquito net as well.

Dusk and the hours of darkness are supposedly the time at which mosquitoes are most active (although they can bite at all times of the day) and it is best to check that your mechanical means of prophylaxis are taken or applied at this time in particular. To really be on the safe side wear clothing with long sleeves and trouser legs, as well as socks if possible, though you might have to weigh the inconvenience of wearing such clothing in the hottest part of the year against the perceived risk of contracting malaria.

Treatment

Treatment usually consists of a course of tablets taken over a three-day period. The tablets, which are obtainable from pharmacies in Malawi, contain powerful ingredients which can have mildly unpleasant side-effects. Once started, the treatment must be followed to the end as failure to do so will result in the body's reduced resistance to the disease should it be contracted again.

Recovery should be evident within a week after treatment is commenced. However, if the disease is left undiagnosed or untreated then symptoms get progressively more debilitating and certainly life-threatening, which would necessitate admission to hospital for last resort treatment involving the administration of a quinine drip.

Bilharzia (schistosomiasis)

It is wise to assume that all rivers, streams and dams in Malawi are infected with bilharzia. The parasite is present in water in which man, the principal host, has either urinated or defecated. In a country like

Malawi where a large number of the rural villages are undeveloped and situated close to water courses, it is inevitable that people will swim and play in streams, which would result in their contamination.

Bilharzia is also present at the lakeshore, and a good indication as to which areas are more likely to be contaminated is the presence of reeds and other vegetation growing in the water. This is because the water snail that is the intermediate host of the bilharzia parasite depends on the vegetation for its survival.

Symptoms

The first clues to possible infection may be noticeable a few hours after swimming in infected water. These consist of a slight rash and tingling of the skin at the site where the larvae have entered. These symptoms then subside and a period of up to six weeks might elapse before more major symptoms, such as a high temperature, become noticeable. Be aware that it is possible to confuse the fever with malaria.

Instead of fever, the first symptoms to be noticed may be lassitude and malaise. However, once the infection has become well established, the more common and obvious symptoms are signs of blood in the urine and stools accompanied by possible abdominal pain.

Prophylaxis

Apart from not swimming in infected water, protection is afforded by briskly drying oneself and clothing on leaving the water. This is because the minute larvae die quickly when removed from water, nor are they likely to survive and penetrate the skin if rubbed hard with a towel.

Treatment

Treatment consists of taking one tablet only. If the traveller suspects bilharzia on returning home, he should ask his doctor to carry out a stool and urine analysis. However, as the eggs take between 30 and 40 days to develop, any tests done before this period has elapsed are likely to produce negative results.

Sleeping sickness (trypanosomiasis)

This disease, which is transmitted by the bite of an infected tsetse fly, has virtually been eliminated from Malawi but rare cases do occur now and again, especially in the lower Shire area, Liwonde National Park, Kasungu National Park and in Vwaza Marsh Game Reserve.

Symptoms

The first symptom of infection is usually a swelling at the site of the bite, which may resemble a boil. This can develop up to five days after being bitten by an infected tsetse fly.

Fever may develop after two or three weeks and this can be followed by severe illness. A lack of adequate treatment can result in damage to the central nervous system, causing day-time drowsiness, the characteristic from which the disease derives its name.

Prophylaxis/prevention

Avoidance of being bitten by the tsetse fly is the best form of prevention. The fly is brown and about the same size as a common house-fly. She has a pointed proboscis which projects forward from her head and she folds her wings across her back.

The tsetse fly is most active during the day and out of doors. It is attracted to large moving objects, including cars. When in an infested area keep car windows tightly closed and preferably wear clothing that covers most of the body. The fly is extremely stubborn and the best form of killing it is by means of a fly swatter, since even fly sprays and repellent lotions are ineffective.

Treatment

If detected in time and correctly diagnosed, the disease is easily treated.

Rabies (hydrophobia)

As the disease is endemic to Malawi, the government authorities are extremely conscious of the threat presented by the disease and carry out periodic shootings of any stray dogs.

Symptoms

Those who have been bitten by an animal should not wait for symptoms to develop but rather visit a doctor immediately.

Prevention

Stray dogs or cats should never be approached, and it is best to make a special effort to get away from any animal that displays unusual behaviour. "Cute" animals such as squirrels and hedgehogs should be left alone as they may also be carriers of rabies.

Even licks on the skin and other minor forms of exposure such as scratches, abrasions or small bites through clothing should be considered serious enough to report to a doctor.

Treatment

Treatment is administered by means of a course of injections which are effective if given soon after the patient has been bitten.

Tickbite fever

The presence of long grass usually means that ticks will be in the vicinity. Only certain species of tick carry the disease, so if you have been bitten by a tick, it does not necessarily mean that you will contract the disease. Folk wisdom has it that the small red ticks are more likely to be dangerous than the fat grey ones.

Symptoms

An infected bite is usually noticeable by its yellow head with a small black central spot.

The onset of the disease is usually rapid (7–10 days) with symptoms such as severe aching of the bones, headaches, backaches, marked tiredness and glands that become painful and swollen.

Prevention

If you intend walking in the bush you should wear long trousers and socks and keep a look-out for any ticks that could be attached to your clothing.

A tick can be removed by smearing that part of it which is attached to the skin with vaseline or any greasy substance. This will impede the tick's breathing ability and cause it to release its grip, making it easier to pull away when the grease is wiped off. Another means of forcing the tick to loosen its hold on the skin is to hold a lighted cigarette close to its body. By just pulling on the tick without using the above methods, the tick's mouthparts are likely to be left behind, which can result in infection.

Treatment

A course of tetracycline will usually cure the disease.

Scorpions

These are most likely to be encountered while camping in the bush. The more dangerous species are found in areas that are nearer to South Africa.

Prevention

Shake out clothes and empty shoes before putting them on. Be watchful when picking up firewood and when touching loose bark on trees.

Symptoms

A sting is unlikely to cause more than severe local pain, but a few species can produce symptoms such as vomiting, diarrhoea and sweating. The more poisonous scorpion stings affect the heart muscle, causing a drop in blood pressure and possible heart failure.

Treatment

A hospital should be contacted immediately in case an adrenalin injection is needed to counteract a drop in blood pressure which might be experienced by certain hypersensitive individuals. Otherwise local anaesthetic and possibly a powerful analgesic can be used to treat the pain.

Snakes

Of the poisonous snakes the green and black mambas are most prevalent in Malawi. Snakes are more likely to be seen between September and May and although the winter is not cold enough for them to hibernate, they are less active between June and August.

Protection/prevention

Keep your eyes peeled when walking in the bush, especially for the very well-camouflaged puffadders who like lying in pathways. When walking over logs or rocks beware of stepping onto a snake on the other side. Closed shoes and long trousers should also be worn.

If you are confronted by an angry snake you should remain still until it has moved away as snakes are most likely to strike at moving objects.

If you are sleeping out of doors, try raising your bed above the ground to a height of at least 30 cm. A well tucked-in mosquito net or ground-sheet that has been sewn in can also help. You should check the arms and legs of any clothing that has been left hanging up or lying around.

Symptoms

Symptoms vary according to the type of snake that one has been bitten by, therefore instead of waiting for symptoms to develop, take immediate action to get the victim to hospital or to the nearest doctor. If the snake cannot reliably be identified, you could try to kill it and take it to hospital for positive identification. When killing it try to do so without crushing its head, as apart from body markings, identification is carried out by examining the dental structure. Only attempt to kill the snake if you are confident of being able to do so safely and without risking a second bite.

Treatment

The first action that should be taken involves ensuring that the victim remains calm. A number of cases of death caused by snake-bite have been the result of the psychological shock which arises as a result of having been bitten, even by a harmless snake. In addition, keeping the victim calm will ensure that the venom, if any, will not circulate in the bloodstream as quickly as it might have done had the victim been allowed to exert himself.

The bitten limb should be immobilised to further prevent distribution of the venom and the victim should be transported to the nearest hospital with as little movement as possible. If the victim must move, then he should do so slowly. Paracetamol, and not aspirin, should be given for the treatment of pain.

The use of antivenom by persons without medical knowledge is discouraged as certain patients might be adversely affected by it. No attempts should be made to suck out the venom, nor should cuts be made at the site of the bite. Neither should ice be applied to the bite nor tourniquets used unless the snake has been positively identified as a cobra or mamba. In this case a pressure pad can be applied to the wound or a firmly tied crepe bandage can be wrapped around the bitten limb between the site of the bite and the heart.

Other illnesses and ailments

AIDS/venereal diseases

Casual sexual contact with the local populace should be avoided as both AIDS and other venereal diseases are widespread.

Blood that is donated for transfusion is usually tested for AIDS and discarded if it is found to be contaminated. Although disposable blood transfusion kits are usually in use in the main centres, you would perhaps be wise to include a few in your luggage. The same applies to syringes and needles.

Diarrhoea

Water in the cities and towns is safe to drink. Safe drinking water is also provided at the various national parks and at lakeshore resorts (except at Stevens' Resthouse and Cape Maclear).

However, if you are camping in more remote areas you should boil the water for at least seven minutes to be sure of killing any harmful bacteria. Sterilising tablets are also effective.

The change in drinking water from that to which you are accustomed can cause a condition that could be called "traveller's diarrhoea", but this is usually short-lived and not serious. A supply of anti-diarrhoeal tablets can prove to be useful in such an instance, for practical reasons, although doctors recommend that the body be allowed to fight the bug in its own way.

Most cases of diarrhoea pass within 48–72 hours without treatment, but if the stools contain blood or diarrhoea lasts more than ten days, a doctor should be contacted. If vomiting and diarrhoea are so severe that even water can't be kept down, then you should see a doctor as soon as possible.

The most important first-aid measure you can take involves keeping up adequate fluid intake. You can easily make a home-made rehydration solution by adding half a teaspoon of salt and four heaped teaspoons of sugar to one litre of boiled water.

You should take care when preparing foodstuffs for eating purposes. Fruit and vegetables should always be washed very well and you should also avoid buying fresh meat at open markets. If fresh fish is to be eaten, it should be odourless and if the gill flaps are lifted with a finger, the gills should be pink.

Putsi fly

All clothes dried in the open air must be thoroughly ironed before they are worn. The putsi fly lays its eggs in damp clothing especially if it bears traces of urine or sweat. The eggs lie dormant in the clothing until they come into contact with the warmth of the wearer's skin, when they hatch. Larvae emerge and burrow into the skin where they grow to full size.

Indication of a putsi's presence is usually skin that is irritated, raised and itchy, possibly resembling a boil in appearance with a small black dot in the centre. The maggot can be forced to emerge from the skin by smearing vaseline over the site and gently squeezing it. But if it does not emerge, vaseline should be reapplied, possibly under a plaster to prevent it being accidentally rubbed off. This will inhibit the putsi's ability to breathe and it should emerge on its own after a day or two.

After it has emerged from the skin the area should be bathed in antiseptic cream or lotion.

Even though it sounds awful, you will be none the worse for wear as the result of the experience although a slight scar may remain. However, if the skin in the genital region is penetrated, it might prove to be far more abhorrent!

The putsi fly is generally active during the hotter months of the year (October to April) and is most likely to be found in the region of fruit trees.

SAFETY PRECAUTIONS

Apart from any other precautions mentioned in previous sections of the book, the following should be considered.

The bush

Public campsites in the National Parks are not fenced and there are no facilities where children can play without constant supervision of adults. Walking in the bush is permitted if you are accompanied by a game scout. However, even if he is armed, his presence offers no insurance against attack, for instance by a charging elephant or lion.

The lake

Before swimming in the lake, especially at the more remote beaches always ask a local whether hippo have recently been seen in the area.

Never walk outside or swim after sunset and before sunrise. It might be worth extending these deadlines to from the late afternoon to early morning.

Getting lost/breaking down

Malawi is a small and densely populated country and even if you do get lost, it should not be long before a passerby comes along. The same applies to breaking down. However, to avoid the possibility of being stranded in a national park or on Mulanje, inform the authorities in the area of the places that you are planning to visit, and your estimated time of return to the camp or starting point. If in a national park never leave your car and attempt to walk back to the main camp.

Wherever you are travelling always try and keep a supply of water in the car especially if children are present. Also endeavour to keep your petrol tank as full as possible.

First-aid kit

If you are planning to travel to the more remote areas a small first-aid manual is useful for information regarding methods of carrying out certain basic actions that might just help save a life in an emergency.

A small first-aid kit packed with items recommended by a pharmacist or doctor who is informed that you are visiting Malawi could also prove to be useful in an emergency.

WHAT TO TAKE

Clothing

For the greater part of the year, i.e. from September to May, a shirt and shorts or trousers for men and a light skirt and blouse for women can be considered adequate. Pack a cardigan for cooler weather and a raincoat or umbrella for the rainy season.

A jersey will provide warmth during the months of June to August. If you are visiting Nyika or Mulanje you are likely to require warm clothing for night-time only between September and May and for both daytime and night-time during June, July and August.

In Malawi it is against the law for women to appear in public in a dress that does not completely cover her knees, nor is it acceptable for a woman to wear shorts or trousers in public. This dress code also applies when a woman is travelling by car in all the cities and towns. Short dresses, trousers and shorts can be worn on Zomba Plateau, Mulanje, on the *Ilala*, in all the national parks and game reserves and at lakeside resorts and private cottages.

The dress limitations do not apply if a woman customarily wears trousers in any religious community to which she belongs, or if she takes part in sports which require the wearing of trousers and shorts.

For men, long hair, which is loosely defined as hair that falls in bulk to the collar, is illegal. To avoid the embarrassment of being asked to cut one's hair on the spot on arrival in Malawi, male visitors are urged to ensure that their hair length conforms to Malawi's regulations prior to arrival.

The wearing of bellbottoms is prohibited (though it is suspected that this regulation applied to the hippies of the 1970s). Nudity or semi-nudity is frowned upon, as is the wearing of revealing clothing by women, such as slit skirts, plunging necklines or fabrics that are transparent.

The wearing of beachwear is permitted at the lake. Also remember to take suntan lotion and sunglasses. Although straw hats are widely and cheaply available, this is not the case as far as sunglasses and suntan lotion are concerned.

In general, informal clothes are worn during the day, but more formal attire, such as a collar and tie for men, is required if one wishes to dine in the smarter hotel restaurants. For safari purposes, dull, sombre colours are useful as they do not draw the same attention to the wearer as do brighter colours.

All clothing that is dried in the open (not indoors) should be thoroughly ironed before being worn so that any putsi fly eggs which may have been laid on the cloth are killed (see page 145).

Shoes

To avoid the obvious hazards such as snakes, scorpions and thorns, do not walk barefoot in the national parks and game reserves.

If you are going to do a lot of walking, sturdy, well-made walking shoes should be worn. They should be "broken in" before being used for long periods so as to lessen the likelihood of blisters being caused when they are worn for the first time.

Should shoes need to be repaired for any reason, there are a number of skilful cobblers who ply their trade in the various markets for very reasonable fees.

Sporting equipment

If you intend to pursue a particular sport which requires specialist equipment, it is wise to bring your own rather than to rely on it being available in Malawi. Should this prove to be a problem, you could consider writing to one of the specialist clubs whose addresses are listed on page 183 to organise the loan of such equipment while in Malawi.

Food and drink

Most basic foodstuffs are available from Malawi's well-stocked supermarkets. This is more so in the larger centres, so if you plan to camp, you should stock up on food supplies before heading for the more remote areas. Note that imported foodstuffs are fairly expensive.

The locally brewed Carlsberg beer and spirits produced in Malawi such as brandy and the renowned Malawi gin are inexpensive when compared with imported spirits and wines.

A large cool-box and ice-packs are very useful for camping purposes, but it might be difficult to find freezing and refrigeration facilities in the more isolated areas.

Camping gear

Items such as tents, ground sheets and sleeping bags are not easily found in the shops, and if a shop does stock them they are likely to be expensive. So it's worth bringing your own camping items.

Cooking utensils

The same information applies to cooking equipment. IGI in Blantyre can refill gas cylinders within a few hours, but if you are in Lilongwe, the cylinders have to be sent to Blantyre for refilling, which results in a delay of up to a week. Remember that camping gas cylinders are prohibited items on aircraft.

7 WHERE TO STAY

ACCOMMODATION IN THE NATIONAL PARKS

Nyika National Park

The park's main camp, Chelinda, has four comfortable self-contained chalets each with two double bedrooms, living room with open fire-place, bathroom and kitchen with refrigerator. There is also a separate block of six double bedrooms and communal bathrooms. At the time of writing, these bathrooms were not in the best of conditions.

Telephone facilities don't exist but radio contact is usually established with headquarters in Lilongwe every morning.

The camp's kitchen and dining room and refrigeration facilities may be used by guests in the block, and camp staff will prepare and cook the guest's own food for a reasonable tip. All drinking water should be boiled before use.

About a kilometre before the camp, a campsite with two shelters, communal latrine and water bowser is available. Firewood is provided. There is also a small cabin in the Juniper Forest which can accommodate four people.

Both petrol and diesel are usually available but you would be wise to fill up your tank at Rumphi before entering the park. There is a small shop at the camp but again, instead of relying on it, rather stock up with provisions either at Mzuzu or Rumphi.

Basic medical facilities are available at Rumphi. (See table on page 154 for reservation details.)

Kasungu National Park

The main camp at Kasungu is Lifupa Lodge, which has twelve thatched rondavels with two beds in each and room for an extra bed. Cots are available on request. The rondavels also have showers and toilets en

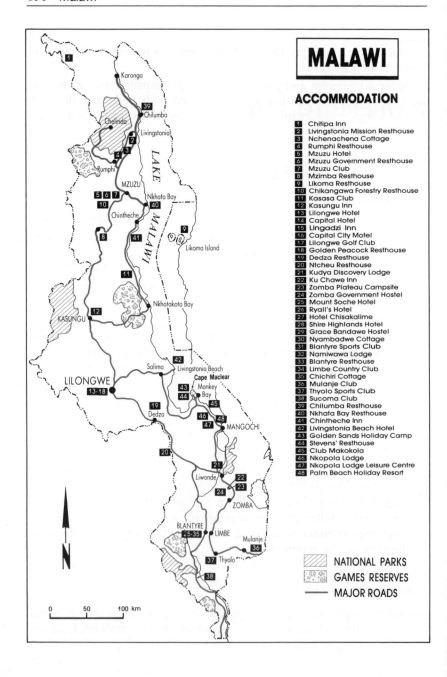

MALAWI

ACCOMMODATION

1 Chitipa Inn
2 Livingstonia Mission Resthouse
3 Nchenachena Cottage
4 Rumphi Resthouse
5 Mzuzu Hotel
6 Mzuzu Government Resthouse
7 Mzuzu Club
8 Mzimba Resthouse
9 Likoma Resthouse
10 Chikangawa Forestry Resthouse
11 Kasasa Club
12 Kasungu Inn
13 Lilongwe Hotel
14 Capital Hotel
15 Lingadzi Inn
16 Capital City Motel
17 Lilongwe Golf Club
18 Golden Peacock Resthouse
19 Dedza Resthouse
20 Ntcheu Resthouse
21 Kudya Discovery Lodge
22 Ku Chawe Inn
23 Zomba Plateau Campsite
24 Zomba Government Hostel
25 Mount Soche Hotel
26 Ryall's Hotel
27 Hotel Chisakalime
28 Shire Highlands Hotel
29 Grace Bandawe Hostel
30 Nyambadwe Cottage
31 Blantyre Sports Club
32 Namiwawa Lodge
33 Blantyre Resthouse
34 Limbe Country Club
35 Chichiri Cottage
36 Mulanje Club
37 Thyolo Sports Club
38 Sucoma Club
39 Chilumba Resthouse
40 Nkhata Bay Resthouse
41 Chintheche Inn
42 Livingstonia Beach Hotel
43 Golden Sands Holiday Camp
44 Stevens' Resthouse
45 Club Makokola
46 Nkopola Lodge
47 Nkopola Lodge Leisure Centre
48 Palm Beach Holiday Resort

▨ NATIONAL PARKS
▨ GAMES RESERVES
— MAJOR ROADS

suite. The lodge has a central restaurant, lounge and cosy bar which overlook the picturesque Lifupa Dam, home to a number of hippo and a variety of waterfowl.

Under a kilometre away from Lifupa is a campsite with seven permanent two- and three-bed tents equipped with beds and linen. A central ablution block and kitchen is provided at the campsite and can be used both by campers and by visitors staying in the rondavels who prefer to prepare their own meals. You should be able to provide your own food which can be prepared by the camp staff for a reasonable tip.

Campers should note that hippos frequent the area as the site overlooks the Ljfupa Dam. The camp also has a resident tame elephant known as Charlie who, despite his apparent tameness, should be treated as a wild animal. It is also advisable that strong-smelling fruit or other food should not be left in one's car or tent as he is likely to investigate the source of the smell with possibly disastrous results.

If accommodation is not available at the camp then your best alternative is at the Kasungu Inn Motel in Kasungu.

Petrol is available at Lifupa Lodge and diesel can be purchased at the administration camp about 4 km away. To be on the safe side however, rather stock up with fuel at Kasungu before entering the park. There are no shopping facilities in the park.

If it is not being used for official duties, a passenger vehicle may be available for hire at the lodge.

(See table on page 154 for reservation details.)

Lake Malawi National Park

No specific visitor facilities have yet been established in the park. However, the run-down Golden Sands Holiday Camp at Cape Maclear has a number of very basic rondavels for hire as well as a campsite. Each rondavel has a toilet with or without running water depending on whether the generator is working. The electrical supply also depends on the state of the generator.

Golden Sands is due to be demolished and a hotel built in its place but there are no clues as to when this will take place.

You may also consider staying at Stevens' Resthouse, where simple food, beers and cold drinks are available. The resthouse is adjacent to a large traditional fishing village and is very popular with backpackers from all over the world.

Hotel accommodation is available at Club Makokola or Nkopola Lodge about 40 km to the south along the lakeshore road (see section on hotels, pages 171/172).

Petrol and diesel are both available at Monkey Bay, which also has medical facilities, a post office and a well-stocked supermarket. Golden Sands has a telephone, which may or may not be working.

(For reservation details see table on page 154.)

Liwonde National Park

Simple accommodation is available at Mvuu Camp, consisting of a number of attractive thatched rondavels in a very pleasant situation on the banks of the Shire River. The camp is served by an ablution block and visitors must provide their own food, cooking utensils and bedding. Firewood is supplied by camp staff.

There are also shops, telephone and petrol and diesel facilities at nearby Liwonde or at the village on the Barrage.

(For reservation details see table on page 154.)

If you prefer hotel accommodation you can stay at the Kudya Discovery Lodge which, although it is outside the National Park, also overlooks the Shire River (see hotels, page 163).

Lengwe National Park

Three chalets are available at the park, each with two double bedrooms and mosquito-gauzed veranda. Additional beds can be put on the veranda if required. Visitors must bring their own food, which will be cooked by staff in the camp's fully equipped kitchen.

There is a well-stocked supermarket at nearby Nchalo where diesel and petrol are also available. Medical facilities are available at the clinic just before Nchalo.

Accommodation is also available at Sucoma, the large sugar-cane plantation which has its entrance gates in Nchalo. Accommodation facilities consist of comfortable air-conditioned chalets in the grounds of the clubhouse, where meals can be purchased. The clubhouse is on the banks of the Shire River and a swimming-pool, tennis and squash courts are available for use by visitors. It must be stressed that Sucoma's chalet facilities are not really geared nor intended for regular and plentiful tourist traffic.

Mulanje

Six forestry huts are situated on the massif's different plateaux. They are reserved for the use of walkers and climbers and can be booked through the Principal Forest Officer.

The huts are equipped with "hard" furniture such as tables, chairs and bunk beds and the Mulanje Mountain Club has a locker in each hut containing a variety of items which would help make a stay in the hut more comfortable. The equipment is for use by members of the Mountain Club, and is also available for use by non-members if prior arrangements are made with the Mountain Club. This can be done by writing to the Club Secretary (for details see page 156).

Alternatively, you could camp at the Mulanje Club, which is at the foot of the massif just past the village of Mulanje. Campers at the club have access to ablution facilities as well as meals.

There are some small shops in Mulanje itself as well as basic medical facilities at the offices of the Red Cross. Petrol and diesel are available at the village as well as telephone facilities.

(See table on page 156 for reservation details.)

Zomba

A secluded campsite with an ablution block is situated on the plateau. Hotel accommodation is available at the Ku Chawe Inn, perched on the edge of the plateau.

In Zomba itself there is the Government Hostel (formerly the Old Residency, see page 163) which offers a reasonable standard of accommodation. Shops, petrol station, post office and medical facilities are also available in Zomba. (See table on page 156 for reservation details.)

ACCOMMODATION IN AND NEAR TO THE NATIONAL PARKS, GAME RESERVES, ZOMBA AND MULANJE

Note: This table is organised in such a way as to provide ready information for those who specifically wish to visit the national parks, game reserves and the hiking areas of Mulanje and Zomba.

Accommodation within the specific area of interest is listed first and this is followed by suggested alternative accommodation supplying reasonable access to the area of interest. This means that certain items have been duplicated from the table on page 157.

Consult the map on page 150 to help you identify the exact location of both numbered and lettered accommodation sources listed below.

Destination	Accommodation	Reservations
Nyika National Park	(A) Chelinda Camp (in park)	Chief Parks and Wildlife Officer, P.O. Box 30131, Lilongwe 3. Tel: 730–853/730–944
	(3) Nchenachena Cottage	Nchenachena Cottage, P.O. Box 30310, Chichiri, Blantyre 3. Tel: 633–551
Kasungu National Park	(B) Lifupa Lodge (in park)	Chief Parks and Wildlife Officer, P.O. Box 30131, Lilongwe 3. Tel: 730–853/730–944
	(12) Kasungu Inn	P.O. Box 48, Kasungu. Tel: 253–306
Lake Malawi National Park	(43) Golden Sands Holiday Camp (in park)	Chief Parks and Wildlife Officer, P.O. Box 30131, Lilongwe 3. Tel: 730–853/730–944
	(44) Stevens' Resthouse	P.O. Box 21, Monkey Bay. Tel: 0–1309
	(45) Club Makokola	P.O. Box 454, Blantyre. Tel: 584–244
	(46) Nkopola Lodge and Leisure Centre	P.O. Box 14, Mangochi. Tel: 584–444
	(48) Palm Beach Holiday Camp	P.O. Box 46, Mangochi. Tel: 620–834
Liwonde National Park	(C) Mvuu Camp (in park)	Chief Parks and Wildlife Officer, P.O. Box 30131, Lilongwe 3. Tel: 730–853/730–944

Destination		Accommodation	Reservations
	(20)	Kudya Discovery Lodge	Private Bag 4, Liwonde. Tel: 532–333/532–481
	(45)	Club Makokola	P.O. Box 454, Blantyre. Tel: 584–244
	(46) + (47)	Nkopola Lodge and Leisure Centre	P.O. Box 14, Mangochi. Tel: 584–444
Lengwe National Park	(D)	Lengwe Camp chalets (in park)	Chief Parks and Wildlife Officer, P.O. Box 30131, Lilongwe 3. Tel: 730–853/730–944
	(38)	Sucoma, Nchalo chalets	Private Bag 50, Blantyre. Tel: 428–200
Vwaza Marsh Game Reserve	(E)	Vwaza Marsh Camp (in reserve)	Chief Parks and Wildlife Officer, P.O. Box 30131, Lilongwe 3. Tel: 730–853/730–944
	(4)	Rumphi Resthouse	Private Bag 22, Rumphi. Tel: 372–251
Nkhotakhota Game Reserve	(F)	Bua and Tongoli camps (in reserve)	Chief Parks and Wildlife Officer, P.O. Box 30131, Lilongwe 3. Tel: 730–853/730–944
	(11)	Dwangwa Kasasa Club	P.O. Box 46, Dwangwa. Tel: 295–266
Majete Game Reserve	(G)	Majete Camp (in reserve)	Chief Parks and Wildlife Officer, P.O. Box 30131, Lilongwe 3. Tel: 730–853/730/944
	(38)	Sucoma Club (at Nchalo)	Private Bag 50, Blantyre. Tel: 428–200

Destination	Accommodation	Reservations
Mwabvi Game Reserve	(H) Mwabvi Camp (in reserve)	Chief Parks and Wildlife Officer, P.O. Box 30131, Lilongwe 3. Tel: 730–853/730–944
	(38) Sucoma Club	Private Bag 50, Blantyre. Tel: 428–200
Mulanje Massif	Mountain huts (on mountain)	The Principal Forester, P.O. Box 50, Mulanje.
	Mulanje Mountain Club facilities	The Secretary, P.O. Box 240, Blantyre.
	(36) Mulanje Club (camping)	P.O. Box 59, Mulanje. Tel: 465–260
Zomba Plateau	(23) Campsite (on plateau)	The Forestry Officer, P.O. Box 29, Zomba. Tel: 523–399
	(22) Ku Chawe Inn (on plateau)	P.O. Box 71, Zomba. Tel: 522–342
	(24) Government Hostel (in town)	P.O. Box 98, Zomba. Tel: 522–688

HOTELS, RESTHOUSES AND CAMPSITES

For convenience, accommodation facilities are divided into Northern, Central and Southern Regions. There is also a separate section for accommodation facilities available at the lakeshore. As far as possible, each establishment is listed in order from north to south within each section.

Each establishment is numbered and its position indicated on the accompanying map. The reader should also consult the more detailed maps of the Lilongwe and Blantyre/Limbe areas on pages 7 and 13.

Tariffs and extra charges

An extra 10 per cent service charge and 10 per cent government tax are charged on top of restaurant, bar and accommodation tariffs. A portion of the revenue arising from the service charge is allocated to the Hotel Training School in Blantyre for the improvement of training facilities, while the remainder is distributed among hotel and restaurant staff.

Tariffs are ranked as high, medium or low, a classification which is related to charges within Malawi only.

Resthouses

It is wise to assume that all resthouses are pretty basic, but they do serve a purpose in that they provide a reasonably priced roof over your head. This means that you can anticipate having the use of a bed, with or without bedding; the use of running water and access to a kitchen where you can either cook your own food or arrange for it to be cooked for you. You should supply all your own food and drink.

Street addresses for the majority of resthouses have been omitted as many of the more rural areas do not have street names. Most passersby in the street will be able to inform you of the location of the resthouse. Most resthouses are located within easy reach of the *boma* or government administration offices. Note that several resthouses permit camping within their grounds.

Private clubs

Malawi has privately run clubs in a number of places, some of which have camping facilities. Even if you would prefer not to camp at the club you could still take out temporary (daily) membership which grants access to the club's sporting and other facilities.

NORTHERN REGION

Chitipa
(1) Chitipa Inn
Tariff: Low   P.O. Box 1, Chitipa. Tel: 382-228

Livingstonia Plateau
(2) Livingstonia Mission Resthouse
Tariff: Low   P.O. Livingstonia. Tel: 368-223

Accommodation	Facilities	Attractions/Activities
Stone House	Basic medical care	Mission buildings
Booking advisable	Fuel	Khondowe rock shelter
	Basic repairs	Magnificent view
		Picnics
		Manchewe Falls

Simple but comfortable accommodation is available in the Old Stone House situated within the mission grounds. Constructed in 1903 by Dr Robert Laws, who was responsible for the establishment and development of the Mission, the house's thick stone walls were built from material cut from a nearby quarry.

Visitors should supply their own food which can be prepared by staff on the premises for a small but reasonable tip.

Nchenachena

(3) Nchenachena Cottage
Tariff: Low   P.O. Box 30310, Chichiri, Blantyre 3. Tel: 633-551

Accommodation	*Facilities*	*Attractions/Activities*
Cottage	Visitors' food	Useful stopover
Booking advisable	prepared for a small tip	Walks in foothills

The cottage has five double rooms with electricity and piped water. Situated on the S86 between Livingstonia and Rumphi on the foothills of the Nyika Plateau, this is a useful stopover place if other establishments such as Nyika's Chelinda Camp or Livingstonia Mission are full. Note that it is not within the national park boundaries and a road distance of about 85 km separates Nchenachena from the park.

Rumphi

(4) Rumphi Resthouse
Tariff: Low   Private Bag 22, Rumphi. Tel: 372-251

Mzuzu

(5) Mzuzu Hotel
Tariff: High   P.O. Box 231, Mzuzu. Tel: 332-622, Telex: 4853

Accommodation	*Facilities*	*Attractions/Activities*
Hotel	Licensed restaurant	Base for visit to
Booking advisable	Shop	Nkhata Bay,
	Telephone	Chintheche
		Viphya Plateau

This is a modern hotel mainly used by business travellers during the week. It serves as a useful base for visits to surrounding areas.

(6) Mzuzu Government Resthouse
Tariff: Low   Laws Avenue, P.O. Box 10, Mzuzu. Tel: 332-219

(7) Mzuzu Club
Tariff: Low   P.O. Box 45, Mzuzu. Tel: 335-040

Situated next door to Mzuzu Hotel, the club offers camping accommodation, basic meals six days a week, as well as tennis and golfing facilities.

Mzimba

(8) Mzimba Resthouse
Tariff: Low   P.O. Box 8, Mzimba. Tel: 342-255

Likoma Island

(9) Likoma Resthouse, on beach
Tariff: Low   P.O. Box 1, Likoma. Tel: 352-211

Chikangawa

(10) Chikangawa Forestry Resthouse
Tariff: Low   P.O Chikangawa. Tel: 332-413/332-477

The resthouse is situated on the edge of the forest at Chikangawa just off the main road to Mzuzu. Cooking utensils are supplied but you should bring your own food and drink. Resthouse staff will assist you in preparing your meals.

CENTRAL REGION

Dwangwa

(11) Kasasa Club, Dwangwa Sugar Corporation.
Tariff: Low   P.O. Box 46, Dwangwa. Tel: 295-266

Accommodation	Facilities	Attractions/Activities
Self-catering	Swimming-pool	Beautiful beach
chalets	Squash court	Crocodile farm
Booking essential	Tennis courts	Nkhotakota Game
	9 hole golf-course	Reserve
	Restaurant/pub	

The club is run by the Dwangwa Sugar Corporation and the grounds contain a number of self-catering chalets that each sleep four to six people in comfort. The chalets are available at a reasonable rental but prior booking is essential as preference is given to employees.

It's worth eating at the clubhouse mess as the food is plentiful, wholesome and cheap, although each chalet has cooking and refrigeration facilities.

The club is situated about 10 km from the lake, where employees of the sugar estate have a number of private cottages. If you can organise it with the manager, you may be able to use the beach which is, not surprisingly, very much an embodiment of tropical paradise.

Adjacent to the estate's grounds is Nkhotakota Game Reserve. A stay at the club could be combined with daily visits to the reserve if you prefer not to camp.

Kasungu

(12) Kasungu Inn
Tariff: Low   P.O. Box 48, Kasungu. Tel: 253-306

As part of the chain of government resthouses the Inn is not the most luxurious of places although it does offer meals and bar facilities. Its situation is handy for those who wish to visit Kasungu National Park (if accommodation within the park is fully booked) or Kamuzu Academy.

Lilongwe

(13) Lilongwe Hotel
Tariff: High   Kamuzu Procession Road, P.O. Box 44, Lilongwe.
Tel: 721-866, Telex: 4321

Accommodation	*Facilities*	*Attractions/Activities*
Hotel	Swimming-pool	Access to Lilongwe
Booking essential	Restaurants	
	Bar	
	Curio shop	
	Taxis	
	Hairdressers	

The hotel is centrally situated in the Old Town section of Lilongwe. All its rooms have private bath and shower.

(14) Capital Hotel
Tariff: High   P.O. Box 30018, Capital City, Lilongwe 3. Tel: 730-444, Telex: 44892

Accommodation	*Facilities*	*Attractions/Activities*
Hotel	Swimming-pool	Access to Lilongwe
Booking essential	Restaurants	
	Bars	
	Taxis	
	Coachline stop	
	Car hire	
	Squash courts	
	Curio shop	
	Bank	
	Hairdressing	

Reputed to be Malawi's top hotel, the international-standard Capital Hotel nestles in the privacy of carefully tended parkland a few hundred metres away from New Town's city centre.

(15) Lingadzi Inn
Tariff: Medium/high   Chilambula Road, P.O. Box 30367, Lilongwe. Tel: 720-644, Telex: 4321

Accommodation	*Facilities*	*Attractions/Activities*
Hotel	Restaurant	Access to Lilongwe
	Bar	

The Lingadzi Inn is a little out of the mainstream of things but still well situated for easy car access to Lilongwe. It is more popular with local visitors than with foreign tourists.

(16) Capital City Motel
Tariff: Medium   P.O. Box 30454, Lilongwe 3. Tel: 733-966

Accommodation	*Facilities*	*Attractions/Activities*
Motel	Restaurant	Access to Lilongwe
	Bar	

The hotel is a bit difficult to find as it is off the beaten track. However it is fairly near to New Town and is on the same road as the Capital City Nursery in Area 13. Like the Lingadzi Inn it attracts a mostly local clientele.

(17) Lilongwe Golf Club
Tariff: Low   P.O. Box 160, Lilongwe. Tel: 720-292

Accommodation	*Facilities*	*Attractions/Activities*
Camping	Ablution	Access to Lilongwe
	Meals	Good place to
	Bars	meet expatriate
	Darts	residents and
	Snooker	backpackers
	Tennis	
	Squash	
	Swimming	

Lilongwe Golf Club, which was formerly the site of Lilongwe's first hospital, boasts the only 18 hole golf-course in the country. Its camping site is also extremely popular with the steady stream of backpackers and overlanders that find their way to the Capital City *en route* through Malawi.

(18) Golden Peacock Resthouse
Tariff: Low   Johnstone Road, Area 3, P.O. Box 793, Lilongwe. (Note: The manager does not accept written bookings.) Tel: 722-002/723-152

Accommodation	*Facilities*	*Attractions/Activities*
Resthouse	Separate shower and	Access to Lilongwe
Booking advisable	toilet	Excellent Indian
	Restaurant	restaurant attached
		Good place to meet
		other travellers

The resthouse is clean and well-run and set in park-like gardens in a residential area just above Lilongwe's Old Town. Its Indian restaurant offers excellent, reasonably priced curries which are very popular with residents. Conventional food is also available at the restaurant.

Dedza

(19) Dedza Resthouse
Tariff: Low   P.O. Box 108, Dedza. Tel: 220-201

Ntcheu

(20) Ntcheu Resthouse
Tariff: Low   Private Bag 1, Ntcheu. Tel: 235-411

SOUTHERN REGION

Liwonde

(21) Kudya Discovery Lodge
Tariff: Medium/high   P/Bag 4, Liwonde. Tel: 532-333, Telex: 4327

Accommodation	*Facilities*	*Attractions/Activities*
Motel	Swimming-pool	Liwonde National Park
Booking advisable	Bar	Shire River
	Restaurant	Cruise
	Telephone	
	Camping	

The lodge is in a superb location overlooking the Shire River whose resident hippos are easily seen. It provides easy access to Liwonde National Park and useful alternative accommodation to Mvuu Camp in the park.

Zomba

(22) Ku Chawe Inn
Tariff: High   Zomba Plateau. P.O. Box 71, Zomba. Tel: 522-342, Telex: 4795

Accommodation	*Facilities*	*Attractions/Activities*
Hotel	Restaurant	Zomba Plateau
Booking essential	Bar	Horseriding
		Walks
		Trout fishing

The hotel is fairly old, but being situated on the edge of the plateau, it boasts a marvellous view. Ku Chawe Inn is an excellent base for exploring the Zomba Plateau.

(23) Zomba Plateau Campsite
All enquiries to be made to Ku Chawe Inn Hotel.

The campsite is situated a little further along the road past the hotel. It has ablution facilities and offers the same access to the plateau as the hotel.

(24) Zomba Government Hostel
Tariff: Low/medium   P.O. Box 98, Zomba. Tel: 522-688

The hostel consists of the modernised shell of one of the first buildings to be constructed in Zomba. It offers reasonable accommodation and restaurant facilities.

Blantyre

(25) Mount Soche Hotel
Tariff: High   Victoria Avenue, P.O. Box 284, Blantyre. Tel: 620-588,
Telex: 4618

Accommodation	*Facilities*	*Attractions/Activities*
Hotel	Restaurants	Immediate access to
Booking essential	Bars	Blantyre
	Swimming-pool	
	Curio shop	
	Taxis	

Facilities at the Mount Soche can be rated on a par with those of the Capital Hotel in Lilongwe although the latter, being newer, is more modern.

The Michiru Room restaurant on the top floor of the hotel is said to offer the best dining fare in Malawi.

The hotel is very centrally situated at the top end of Blantyre's main shopping avenue.

(26) Ryall's Hotel
Tariff: High   Hannover Avenue, P.O. Box 21, Blantyre. Tel: 620-955, Telex: 44481

Accommodation	*Facilities*	*Attractions/Activities*
Hotel	Restaurant	Immediate access to
Booking essential	Bar	Blantyre
	Swimming-pool	
	Curio shop	
	Taxis	

Just around the corner from the Mount Soche, the recently refurbished Ryall's Hotel is also a stone's throw away from Blantyre's city centre.

The 21 Grill restaurant vies with the Mount Soche for the distinction of being Malawi's top restaurant.

(27) Hotel Chisakalime
Tariff: Medium   Tsiranana Road, P.O. Box 5249, Limbe. Tel: 652-266

Accommodation	Facilities	Attractions/Activities
Hotel	Restaurant	Swinging nightclub
Booking advisable	Bar	where one can get to
	Nightclub	meet the locals
	Cinema	

Situated closer to Limbe than to Blantyre, the Chisakalime is an unpretentious little hotel whose main claim to fame is its Zikomo Nightclub, which is usually packed on Friday and Saturday nights.

(28) Shire Highlands Hotel
Tariff: Medium   Churchill Road, P.O. Box 5204, Limbe. Tel: 640-055, Telex: 4481

Accommodation	Facilities	Attractions/Activities
Hotel	Restaurant	Close to Limbe
Booking advisable	Bar	Tobacco auction floors
	Swimming-pool	Society of Malawi and
		proposed railway museum
		across the road

Very reminiscent of colonial days, the ageing hotel is set in mature gardens that feature a pleasant swimming-pool. The hotel is popular with the migrant tobacco buyers who for half the year conduct their trade at the Limbe Tobacco auction floors just a few hundred metres down the road.

(29) Grace Bandawe Hostel
Tariff: Low   Chileka Road, P.O. Box 1096, Blantyre. Tel: 650-046
This is a good, clean, low-cost alternative to the hotels. Simple meals are provided by the hostel's canteen.

(30) Nyambadwe Cottage
Tariff: Low/medium   Nyambadwe Crescent, P.O. Box 30310, Chichiri, Blantyre 3. Tel: 633-551
This establishment is a little off the beaten track but still close to Blantyre. It offers a good breakfast and snacks if requested, in clean surroundings.

(31) Blantyre Sports Club
Tariff: Low   Off Victoria Avenue, P.O. Box 245, Blantyre. Tel: 635-173

Accommodation	*Facilities*	*Attractions/Activities*
Camping	Restaurant	Immediate access to
	Ablution	Blantyre
	Golf-course	Good cheap food
	Aerobics	Useful place for meeting
	Squash	expatriate residents.
	Tennis	
	Swimming	
	Snooker	
	Bowls	
	Entertainment	

The Blantyre Sports Club's reasonably priced restaurant is very popular with local residents. The club offers campers an excellent base for access to the heart of Blantyre.

(32) Namiwawa Lodge
Tariff: Low/medium   Follow signposts off Chilomoni Ring Road, P.O. Box 30310, Chichiri, Blantyre 3. Tel: 633-551
This is a converted house situated in a residential area close to Blantyre.

(33) Blantyre Resthouse
Tariff: Low   P.O. Box 1116, Blantyre. Tel: 634-460
The resthouse can be reached by taking the first turnoff to the right after passing under the railway bridge at the start of Chileka Road.

Remember to ask for the executive suite which offers superior accommodation.

(34) Limbe Country Club
Tariff: Low   Off Churchill Road, P.O. Box 5031, Limbe. Tel: 641-022

Accommodation	*Facilities*	*Attractions/Activities*
Camping	Ablution	Close to Limbe
	Restaurant	Good place to meet
	Bar	expatriate residents
	Tennis	Good cheap food
	Bowls	
	Golf	
	Snooker	
	Swimming	
	Squash	

The club is not geared up with a camping site as such but club officials say they will accommodate campers on request.

(35) Chichiri Cottage
Tariff: Low/medium   Off Kamuzu Highway on Blantyre side of Independence Arch, P.O. Box 30310, Chichiri, Blantyre 3. Telephone: 633-551.

Mulanje

(36) Mulanje Club
Tariff: Low   P.O. Box 59, Mulanje. Tel: 465-260

Accommodation	*Facilities*	*Attractions/Activities*
Camping	Meals	Good access to
	Bar	Mulanje Massif
	Tennis	
	Squash	
	Golf	

The Mulanje Club offers useful alternative camping accommodation for those who wish to explore Mulanje without staying in the huts on the mountain itself.

For daytrippers from Blantyre, a cold "Green" on the club's *khonde* which lies at the foot of the towering bulk of Mulanje offers a very pleasant interlude.

If you wish to eat at the club, meals must be ordered an hour or two in advance.

Thyolo

(37) Thyolo Sports Club
Tariff: Low   P.O. Box 44, Thyolo. Tel: 472-259

Set in the midst of the tea estates, the very least that the club offers is a wonderful cup of tea. There are no camping facilities, but the management might be persuaded to allow you to pitch your tent within the club grounds, which feature a swimming-pool, tennis court, golf-course and squash court.

Nchalo

(38) Sucoma Club
Tariff: Low   Private Bag 50, Blantyre. Tel: 428-200

This estate is part of the same Sugar Corporation and the set-up is similar to that of the Kasasa Club in Dwangwa, further north.

Situated in the lower Shire Valley at Nchalo, the club offers chalets at reasonable rental just off the banks of the fast flowing Shire River.

This is a good base for a visit to Lengwe National Park or Mwabvi Game Reserve.

Sporting facilities include tennis, squash, swimming, fishing and the clubhouse offers bar and basic meal facilities.

If you feel like a trip on the Shire River, ask the boatman to take you on the noisy "Poopdeck" launch which is sometimes anchored on the river just adjacent to the swimming-pool and chalet area.

THE LAKESHORE

NORTHERN REGION

Chilumba

(39) Chilumba Resthouse, a few hundred metres from the jetty
Tariff: Low   Tel: 364-225

Nkhata Bay

(40) Nkhata Bay Resthouse
Tariff: Low   P.O. Box 1, Nkhata Bay. Tel: 352-249

Chintheche

(41) Chintheche Inn
Tariff: Medium   P.O. Chintheche. Tel: Chintheche 11, Telex: 4645

Accommodation	*Facilities*	*Attractions/Activities*
Motel	Restaurant	Beautiful beach
Booking advisable	Bar	Bandawe Mission Site
		Nkhata Bay

The main attraction of this fairly remote place is its beautiful beach. At present the inn is fairly small and offers simple fare but there may be plans to privatise and upgrade it.

CENTRAL REGION

Senga Bay

(42) Livingstonia Beach Hotel

Tariff: High   P.O. Box 11, Salima. Tel: 261-422, Telex: 4148

Accommodation	*Facilities*	*Attractions/Activities*
Hotel	Restaurant	Parasailing
Booking essential	Bar	Windsurfing
Camping	Swimming-pool	Sailing
	Barbecues	Skiing
		Walks
		Curios
		Nearest to Lilongwe

The hotel, formerly known as Grand Beach Hotel, had its heyday in the sixties and seventies but was allowed to become run down.

Situated at the end of the M5 from Lilongwe, which is about an hour and a half away by car, the hotel was completely refurbished in 1987 and is now comparable in standard with Club Makokola and Nkopola Lodge. Among other attractions it features supposedly the largest swimming-pool on the lakeshore and a cosy beach bar.

The owners have also provided facilities for a wide range of water sports. The beach is fairly narrow and unfortunately the sand is sometimes not as white as on other beaches. This is mainly because of the alluvial deposits of titanium and not, as one might think, because of oil pollution washed in from the lake.

It is possible to hire the services of one of the inhabitants from the fishing village just adjacent to the campsite, and be ferried in a dugout to the island facing the hotel. Guides are also available for walks in the Senga Bay Hills just behind the hotel, which although they are not that high up, provide a worthwhile panoramic view of the lake and surrounding land. You can also hire a guide to take you to the hippo swamps on the other side of the hill.

A word of warning about swimming at beaches all along this coastline should be heeded as there have been at least two fatalities caused by hippo in the last few years.

SOUTHERN REGION

Cape Maclear

(43) Golden Sands Holiday Camp

Tariff: Low   Chief Wildlife Officer, P.O. Box 30131, Lilongwe 3. Tel: 730-853/730-944

Accommodation	*Facilities*	*Attractions/Activities*
Rondavels	Possibly bar	Immediate access to
Campsite	Possibly limited meals	Cape Maclear
	Possibly water and electricity	

Golden Sands is signposted off the Mangochi/Monkey Bay Road (M15). The mostly untarred road, which can present problems during the rainy season, should be followed for 19 km to where it ends at Golden Sands.

The resort comprises the seedy remnants of a former luxury establishment. In a way this is a blessing as, although the owners have taken advantage of the prime site within the area, they have not exploited the surroundings in a commercial sense. Somehow, it all blends in with the surroundings without creating a jarring note, or attracting hordes of tourists.

However, plans have been afoot for many years now to develop the site and build a hotel of international standards, but until such time as they actually demolish the complex, it seems Golden Sands will carry on and on.

The complex is not recommended for the visitor who seeks any form of "mod cons" or luxury, but for the person who is prepared to go without running water or electricity (as happens occasionally). The accommodation facilities are adequate and the beach is another little slice of tropical paradise, complete with palm trees.

An added bonus is the proximity of Otter Point, just a short walk away from Golden Sands, where, equipped with just a snorkel, you can explore the shoreline waters, an experience which has been likened to swimming in a giant aquarium (see page 48 for details on Lake Malawi National Park).

(44) Stevens' Resthouse
Tariff: Low   P.O. Box 21, Cape Maclear. Tel: 0-1309

Accommodation	*Facilities*	*Attractions/Activities*
Resthouse	Bar	Good access to Cape
	Limited meals	Maclear
	Possibly water and electricity	

The resthouse is reached by taking the right-hand fork from the road that leads to Golden Sands after the short, tarred hilly section, through the bush and to the fishing village on the lake that is visible in the distance, about a kilometre away. Thereafter, drive through the village along the shoreline and follow the road for a few hundred metres to where it ends at the resthouse.

From the front door of Mr Stevens' Resthouse one could actually throw a shell into the lake. Built on the beach, the simple resthouse exudes a "tomorrow is another day" atmosphere. If his generator is working, then Mr Stevens will be able to sell you the perfect accompaniment to a hot day on the shores of Lake Malawi : a cold Carlsberg Green. Simple meals, which usually feature *chambo*, are available for a reasonable price. The company is cosmopolitan as many backpackers find their way to this secluded part of the lake.

Just a short way away, the road leading to the resthouse passes through a large traditional village which you might find interesting to explore while being stared at or provoked to donate "one tambala" or even "one US dollar" by curious urchins.

Assorted curio sellers, always keen to bargain, usually hang around the resthouse. In this regard it is worth remembering that if you do not have enough money, old items of clothing are always acceptable as a form of currency.

If you do not have transport and prefer not to walk the 18 km back to the main road, Mr Stevens' pickup regularly makes the trip to Monkey Bay.

SOUTHERN LAKESHORE

(45) Club Makokola
Tariff: High   P.O. Box 59, Mangochi. Tel: 584-244, Telex: 4312

Accommodation	*Facilities*	*Attractions/Activities*
Hotel	Restaurant	Beautiful beach
Booking essential	Bar	Cruises
	Barbecue	Snorkelling
	Tennis	Sailing safaris
	Swimming-pool	Waterskiing
	Video room	Windsurfing
	Curio shop	Scuba
	Airstrip	Near to Cape Maclear
	Conferences	

The hotel is about halfway between Mangochi and Monkey Bay on the M15 which is in good condition.

The complex consists of charming thatched cottages set in large grounds and fronted by a magnificent beach. It is extremely popular with foreign tourists, so prior booking is essential.

If you want to spend a few days just soaking up the sun and watching magical sunsets, then this is the place to do it. To burn off any excess energy, there are a variety of watersports in which you can indulge.

The hotel has an interesting curio shop which sells a variety of nick-nacks and for those who want an even broader selection, a number of curio sellers are based under shelter near to the entrance of the hotel grounds.

(46) Nkopola Lodge
Tariff: High   P.O. Box 14, Mangochi. Tel: 584-444, Telex: 44354

Accommodation	*Facilities*	*Attractions/Activities*
Hotel	Restaurant	Beautiful beach
Booking essential	Bar	Sailing safaris
	Video room	Snorkelling
	Curio shop	Windsurfing
	Conferences	Scuba
		Cruises
		Waterskiing
		Near to Cape Maclear

The entrance road that leads to the lodge is off the main road between Mangochi and Club Makokola and is clearly signposted.

The lodge has recently undergone a refurbishment and expansion programme which has included the building of new chalets almost on the resort's superb beach.

As with Club Makokola, the hotel is extremely popular with tourists and prior booking is essential. It also has a curio shop and a group of curio sellers are usually stationed outside the main gate.

If you stay in the rooms that are built into the cliffs overlooking the lake, you are likely to be curiously observed by the voyeuristic monkeys that abound in the area.

(47) Nkopola Lodge Leisure Centre
Tariff: Low/medium   Same address as Nkopola Lodge

Accommodation	Facilities	Attractions/Activities
Bungalows	Ablution	Good beach
Booking advisable	Cooking	Access to hotel's
Camping	Permanent tents	sporting facilities

Nkopola Lodge has a leisure centre near its main hotel which offers the low-budget visitor a number of basic chalets, permanent tents and caravan and tent plots. Each of the permanent tents can accommodate up to six people. There are adequate ablution and cooking facilities. Leisure Centre residents can use the watersport facilities of the main hotel at discounted rates.

(48) Palm Beach Holiday Resort
Tariff: Low/medium   P.O. Box 46, Mangochi. Tel: 620-834

Accommodation	Facilities	Attractions/Activities
Bungalows	Ablution	Fishing
Booking advisable	Cooking	Nature sanctuary
Campsite		Waterskiing
		Windsurfing
		Sailing

A not very obvious sign points in the direction of the resort from the main Mangochi/Monkey Bay Road.

This resort, which is the closest to Mangochi, contains some attractively designed bungalows which each sleep six, and an ablution block. The set-up is likely to suit the more casual holidaymaker who would rather not have to dress up for meals.

Situated at the mouth of the lake's outlet into Lake Malombe and the Shire River, the resort's situation offers plenty of opportunity for birdwatching and fishing.

8 MISCELLANEOUS INFORMATION

Security

From afar it must seem that Malawi is situated in a region that is prone to conflict, what with the Mozambican war that has been raging for over ten years now and the very large influx of Mozambican refugees that are given shelter in the country.

However, you would be making a grave error if the above situation was allowed to influence you against visiting Malawi. There is absolutely no obvious evidence that this situation does exist except for the sizeable collection of makeshift huts housing the refugees, which are noticeable on the roadside at Dedza or further down at Nsanje in the most southerly section of Malawi.

The only warning that you should heed concerning your personal safety would be that you do not travel on the Lilongwe/Blantyre road at night-time. The main road, which passes by Dedza and continues southwards for a distance of approximately 74 km, actually lies on the Mozambique/Malawi border. This is an area where there is a chance that Mozambican soldiers might enter Malawi and stop a passing car in search of money and food.

The other warning to be given concerns travellers who wish to cross from Zimbabwe to Malawi via Tete in Mozambique. A description of the risks that may be encountered by joining the convoy is given on page 98.

Apart from these two possible security risks, Malawi is an extremely peaceful country, a quality which can be attributed to the policies of the Life President, Dr Banda. An impressive aura of harmony between the various races is apparent in everyday encounters, far more so than in most other countries. It is a common occurrence for visitors and residents to be greeted and asked "How are you?" by numerous friendly strangers. This habit of the people of the "warm heart of Africa" has the happy contagious effect of warming one's own heart with Malawi's unique brand of magic.

Banks

The two main banks that conduct business in Malawi are National Bank and Commercial Bank, both of which have a relatively large number of agencies throughout the country.

Banking hours in the larger centres are from Monday to Friday between the hours of 08h00 and 13h00. Banks are closed on Saturdays, Sundays and public holidays. At Kamuzu International Airport the bank is open daily in order to service international flights.

The smaller agencies do not deal in foreign exchange, consequently traveller's cheques should be cashed in the larger centres. The larger hotels are able to cash traveller's cheques but as in other countries, the commission they charge is likely to be higher than that charged in banks.

National Bank of Malawi

Blantyre: Henderson Street
          Victoria Avenue
          Chichiri

Limbe: Churchill Road
        Customs Road

Lilongwe: Capital City
           Old Town

Commercial Bank of Malawi

Blantyre: Victoria Avenue
           Ginnery Avenue

Limbe: Livingstone Avenue

Lilongwe: Capital City
           Old Town

Facilities countrywide

The following table identifies towns which have banking, fuel, hotel or other accommodation, medical, police and grocery shopping facilities.

B = Bank/agency   O = Other accommodation
F = Fuel   P = Police
H = Hotel   S = Supermarket
M = Medical facility

Balaka	B/F/H/O/M/P/S	Mbalachanda	M
Bvumbwe	F/M/O/P	Mchinji	B/F/M/P/S
Chikwawa	B/F/M/P	Migowi	B/M/O/P
Chileka	B/F/M/P/S	Misuku	–
Chilumba	F/M/O/P/S	Mitundu	M
Chintheche	F/H/M/P/S	Mlangeni	M/P
Chipoka	F/O/P	Monkey Bay	B/F/M/O/P/S
Chiradzulu	M/P	Mponela	B/F/M/O/P/S
Chiromo	B/F/M/P/S	Mtakataka	P
Chisemphere	M/S	Mulanje	B/F/M/O/P/S
Chitipa	B/F/M/P/S	Mwanza	M/P/S
Dedza	B/F/M/O/P/S	Mzalangwe	M/P
Domasi	M/O/P	Mzimba	B/F/M/P/S
Dowa	F/M/P	Mzuzu	B/F/H/M/O/P/S
Dwangwa	F/M/O/P/S	Namadzi	F/M/O/P
Ekwendeni	M/S	Nambuma	S
Embangweni	B/M	Namitete	F/M/P/S
Euthini	M/P/S	Namwera	F/P/S
Hora	M/P	Nathenje	O/P/S
Jali	M/O/P/S	Nchalo	B/F/M/O/P/S
Kapiri	–	Ngabu	B/F/M/P/S
Kaporo	M/P	Nkhata Bay	B/F/M/O/P/S
Karonga	B/F/M/O/P/S	Nkhoma	M
Kasiya	P	Nkhotakota	F/M/O/P/S
Kasungu	B/F/H/M/O/P/S	Nsanje	B/M/P/S
Likoma	O/S	Ntaja	B/F/O/P
Linthipe	M/P	Ntcheu	B/F/M/O/P/S
Livingstonia	F/M/O	Ntchisi	F/M/S
Liwonde	B/F/M/O/P/S	Phalombe	B/F/M/P/S
Lizulu	–	Rumphi	F/M/O/P/S
Luchenza	B/F/M/P/S	Ruo	M/P/S
Machinga	M/P	Salima	B/F/M/O/P/S
Madisi	F/S	Sinyala	P
Makwasa	M/O/P/S	Thondwe	M/P/S
Mangochi	B/F/M/O/P/S	Thyolo	B/F/M/O/P/S
Marka	M/P	Ulongwe	M/P
Mbabzi	B/F/M/P/S	Zomba	B/F/H/M/O/P/S

Diplomatic representatives

American Embassy	Lilongwe	730-166
	Blantyre	620-547
British High Commission	Lilongwe	731-544
Chinese Embassy (R.O.C./Taiwan)	Lilongwe	730-611

Egyptian Embassy	Lilongwe	730-300
European Communities	Lilongwe	730-255
French Embassy	Lilongwe	730-579
German Embassy	Lilongwe	731-266
Greek Consulate	Blantyre	631-265
Indian High Commission	Lilongwe	732-700
Irish Embassy	Blantyre	620-960
Israeli Embassy	Lilongwe	731-333
South Korean Embassy	Lilongwe	733-499
Mozambique Embassy	Lilongwe	733-144
Netherlands Consulate	Limbe	651-171
South African Embassy	Lilongwe	730-888
Zambian High Commission	Lilongwe	731-911
Zimbabwe High Commission	Lilongwe	733-988

Entertainment and sport

	Lilongwe	Blantyre	Mzuzu	Zomba
Cinema	*	*		
Theatre	*	*		
Restaurant	*	*	*	*
Golf	*	*	*	*
Squash	*	*		
Tennis	*	*	*	*
Swimming	*	*		

Restaurant facilities are not described in detail owing to the variable nature of this trade. Prospective visitors should be aware that Malawi is not a haven of endless night-time entertainment.

Government offices and hours

Government hours are as follows:

Monday–Friday 07h30–12h00 and 13h00/13h30–16h30/17h00

Government ministries and departments

Ministry/Department	Address	Telephone
Office of the President and Cabinet	P/Bag 388, Capital City, LL3	730-388
Agriculture	Box 30134, Capital City, LL3	733-300
Antiquities	Box 264, Lilongwe	721-844

Ministry/Department	Address	Telephone
Civil Aviation	P/Bag 322, Capital City, LL3	730-122
Customs and Excise	P/Bag 402, Kanengo	765-055
Finance	Box 30049, Capital City, LL3	731-311
Forestry	Box 30048, Capital City, LL3	731-322
Health	Box 30377, Capital City, LL3	730-099
Immigration	Box 331, Blantyre	760-000
Information	Box 179, Lilongwe	720-322
Local Government	Box 30312, Capital City, LL3	732-555
National Archives	Box 62, Zomba	522-922
National Parks and Wildlife	Box 30131, Capital City, LL3	730-944
National Statistical Office	Box 333, Zomba	522-377
Philatelic Bureau	Box 1000, Blantyre	670-778
Police Headquarters	P/Bag 305, Capital City, LL3	733-999
Trade, Industry and Tourism	Box 30366, Capital City, LL3	732-711
Veterinary Services	Box 30372, Capital City, LL3	732-377

Language and customs

Chichewa is the national language but English is the official language and is widely understood.

In general, men are politely addressed as *Bambo*, meaning 'father', and women as *Amai*, which means 'mother'. As most Malawians are interested in asking how one is, it might be useful to remember the phrase *Muli Bwanji?* which means 'how are you?' to which the reply is *Ndili bwino*, meaning 'I am well'. Another useful phrase, meaning 'thank you', is *Zikomo gwambile*.

As stressed elsewhere in the book Malawians are extremely polite, courteous people. In this country anger does not get anyone anywhere. When confronted with anger, the average Malawian is likely to clam up completely. If you are faced with difficulties, patience and a sense of humour will usually win through.

Other useful words and phrases:

Chichewa	English
Moni	Greetings
Chabwino	Good/fine/OK
Pitani bwino	Go well/goodbye
Tsalani bwino	Stay well/goodbye

Chichewa	*English*
Inde	Yes
Iai	No
Chonde	Please
Nyama	Meat
Nsomba	Fish
Mazira	Eggs
Tambala	Cockerel (coin)
Mbatata	Potatoes
Zipatso	Fruit
Madzi	Water
Mkaka	Milk
Kwacha	Dawn (currency note)
Bambo	Father (polite way to address a man)
Amai	Mother (polite way to address a woman)

Petrol and diesel

These are widely available and the price is fixed throughout the country. Diesel is slightly cheaper than petrol. Most filling stations in the larger centres are open from 06h00 to 18h00 while in the rural areas they may close at lunchtime, generally between 12h00 and 13h00.

Public holidays

1 January	New Year's Day
3 March	Martyr's Day
March/April	Easter
14 May	Kamuzu Day
6 July	Republic Day
17 October	Mother's Day
21 December	National Tree Planting Day
25/26 December	Christmas/Boxing day

If a holiday falls on a Saturday or Sunday, the following Monday is declared a holiday. All government offices, banks, businesses and the larger shops are closed over public holidays, although some of the smaller supermarkets may remain open. On Martyr's Day everything is closed and the playing of sport and any form of entertainment is forbidden.

Public transport

See page 106.

Shopping

Shops are generally open from Monday to Friday 07h30/08h00 to 12h00/12h30 (some stores stay open at lunchtime) and 13h00 to 18h00. On Saturdays they open from 08h00 to 12h00 and some of the supermarkets stay open on Saturday afternoons and Sunday.

Most consumer items for daily use can be found in the larger supermarkets. Branches of the PTC (People's Trading Centre) supermarket chain are efficiently run and usually well stocked. They can be found in many of the smaller towns.

Alcohol is sold openly in the supermarkets and there are no separate bottle stores as such.

Now and again there are shortages of certain goods, notably dairy products. As 100 per cent duty is charged on imported items and transport costs, usually from South Africa, are to be included, the goods can be classed as 'expensive'.

The supply of vegetables and fruit varies according to the season. There is a dearth of good quality vegetables during the height of the rainy season, resulting in higher prices.

The following table constitutes a general guideline only for the optimal availability of certain fruits and vegetables. They may be available outside the specified months but their quality and price are not likely to be of the best.

Citrus fruit	May–August
Strawberries	August–October
Pineapples	December–March
Mangoes	November–January
Guavas	March–May
Bananas	All year round
Apples	October–December/imported
Pawpaw	March–December
Grapes	Imported
Peaches	Imported/October–December
Plums	October/November
Mulberries	September
Mushrooms	June/July
Avocadoes	March–May

Tomatoes	June–December
Carrots	May–December
Onions	June–December
Broccoli	July–October
Cauliflower	July–October
Lettuce	April–November
Potatoes	March–December
Green peppers	March–December
Cabbage	All year round
Peas	July–October

(See page 88ff. for notes on souvenir buying and bargaining.)

Although there are always general dealer's stores to be found in the smaller towns and villages in the rural areas, the chances are that they have neither electricity nor refrigeration facilities. Nor are they likely to have as wide a range of goods as are available in the urban areas. Consequently, if you are planning a trip away from the urban areas that will last for a few days or more, it is advisable to buy your provisions in the larger supermarkets.

Although photographic film can be bought in Malawi it is best to bring your own supply of specialist and colour slide film. Certain establishments do process colour film; however, anticipate delays and high prices if using these establishments.

Telephone system

Most of the larger towns in Malawi have automatic telephone exchanges based on a system that generally works quite well. Telephone services that have been disrupted during the rainy season may take some time to be rectified.

Main centre automatic exchange numbers are made up of six digits. Numbers in Lilongwe generally commence with "7" while those in the Blantyre area generally commence with "6".

The hours of operation of manual exchanges in the rural areas are listed in the telephone directory. International calls can be placed at all main centre post offices or from private automatic exchange numbers.

Public telex services exist at post offices in Blantyre and Lilongwe.

Travel agencies and airlines

	Blantyre	Lilongwe	Chileka	KIA	Mzuzu
Air Malawi	620-811	720-966	661-204	760-467	332-644
British Airways	634-002			760-523	
British Caledonian		733-780			
KLM	620-106			760-261	
Kenya Airways	620-820				
SAA	620-629				
UTA French Airlines		732-269			
Air Tanzania		730-732			
Air India	636-051				
Airtour & Travel	635-075				
American Express/Manica	634-533	733-133		760-024	332-638
AMI Press	634-733	730-003			
Budget Travel	634-666				
MTA		721-390			
Soche Tours & Travel	620-777	731-477			

Vehicle hire

See page 104 for details.

Gambling

There are no casinos in Malawi but sometimes casino evenings are held by service organisations such as Lions and Rotary in order to raise funds for charity.

Television, radio and press

As yet there is no television service in Malawi. The MBC (Malawi Broadcasting Corporation) is broadcast on MW, SW and FM in Chichewa and English while news in English is broadcast at 07h00, 18h00 and 20h00 every day and at 12h30 from Monday to Friday.

The national newspaper, the *Daily Times* is published from Monday to Friday in English and covers both international and local news. A weekend newspaper, the *Malawi News* is also published.

International and local magazines and a limited range of books are available at Times Bookshops, branches of which are found in the main centres. Also try Central Bookshop in Blantyre.

The British Council Library has branches in Lilongwe and Blantyre. If you are desperate to read a book or some British newspapers, ask them if you can join the library on a temporary basis.

Electricity

The electrical supply is based on the 220/240 volts system and the three-pin plugs used are of the British 'square bayonet' pin type. Special adaptors are needed for the rounded two-pin types of plugs.

Useful addresses

Conservation

The Wildlife Society (formerly the National Fauna Preservation Society)	P.O. Box 30293, Lilongwe 3.
	P.O. Box 321, Zomba.
	P.O. Box 325, Mzuzu.
	P.O. Box 1429, Blantyre.

Department of Forestry, P.O. Box 30048, Lilongwe 3, Tel: 731-322.

Department of National Parks and Wildlife, P.O. Box 30131, Lilongwe 3, Tel: 723-566, 723-676, 723-505.

Ivory permits obtainable from Department of National Parks and Wildlife offices, P.O. Box 30131 Capital City, Lilongwe 3, Tel: 723-566 or 723-676. The offices are situated in Murray Road, Old Town, Lilongwe.

Tropical Fish Holding Centre, P.O. Box 123, Salima, Tel: 261-261.

Cultural

Society of Malawi (Scientific and Historical), P.O. Box 125, Blantyre.

Museum of Malawi, P.O. Box 30360, Chichiri, Blantyre, Tel: 672-001.

Lake Malawi Museum, P.O. Box 128, Mangochi, Tel: 584-346.

Department of Antiquities, P.O. Box 264, Lilongwe, Tel: 721-844.

Sport

Angling Society of Malawi, P.O. Box 744, Blantyre.

Mulanje Mountain Club, P.O. Box 240, Blantyre.

Ndirande Sailing Club, P.O. Box 422, Blantyre.

Registrar of Firearms, P.O. Box 305, Lilongwe.

Salima Yacht Club, c/o Livingstonia Beach Hotel, P.O. Box 20, Salima.

Yachting Association of Malawi, P.O. Box 402, Blantyre.

Information

SARTOC (Southern African Regional Tourism Council), P.O. Box 564, Blantyre, Tel: 670-722.

Malawi Export Promotion Council, P.O. Box 1299, Blantyre, Tel: 620-499.

Malawi Development Corporation, P.O. Box 566, Blantyre, Tel: 620-100.

Department of Tourism, P.O. Box 402, Blantyre, Tel: 620-300.

Department of Surveys, Map Sales, P.O. Box 349, Blantyre, Tel: 633-722 or P.O. Box 120, Lilongwe, Tel: 720-355.

Secretary of Works and Supplies (for Road Distance Maps and Charts), Private Bag 316, Capital City, Lilongwe 3, Tel: 733-188.

Safaris

Safari Tours, P.O. Box 2075, Blantyre, Tel: 650-003.
Land and Lake Safaris, P.O. Box 30239, Lilongwe 3, Tel: 650-003.

Public transport

United Transport (Malawi) UTM offices where timetables and destination information can be obtained during working hours on weekdays:
Lilongwe: Tel: 720-800
Blantyre: Kamuzu Highway almost opposite the entrance of the Kamuzu Stadium, tel: 671-388

Coachline bookings:
Blantyre: Halls Car Hire and Tours, Hannover Avenue, tel: 620-077
Limbe: Hertz/Coachline offices, Shire Highlands Hotel tel: 640-055.
Lilongwe: Hertz/Coachline desk, Capital Hotel, tel: 731-854 or Coachline Office, UTM Depot, tel: 720-800.

Air/boat charter

Air Charters, P.O. Box 30259, Blantyre, Tel: 620-919.

Rift Lake Charters, P.O. Box 284, Mangochi, Tel: (Club Makokola) 584-244.

Ilala bookings

Malawi Railways Limited, P.O. Box 5492, Limbe, Tel: 640-844 or try Limbe Station, Churchill Road, Limbe.

Medical

Queen Elizabeth Central Hospital, Blantyre, Tel: 630-333.
Kamuzu Central Hospital, Lilongwe, Tel: 721-555.
Seventh Day Adventist Clinic, Tel: 620-006.

Tea estates

British African Tea Estates, Thyolo, Tel: 472-266.
Naming'omba Tea Estates, Thyolo, Tel: 472-346.
Lujenda Tea Estates, Thyolo, Tel: 472-300.
Satemwa Tea Estates, Thyolo, Tel: 472-233.
Conforzi Limited, Thyolo, Tel 472-400.

Places of interest

Carlsberg Breweries (near Blantyre), Tel: 670-377.
Limbe Tobacco Auction Floors, Tel: 640-377.
Livingstonia Mission, P.O. Livingstonia, Tel: 253-448.
Kamuzu Academy, Private Bag, Mtunthama, Tel: 368-223.

Possible source of dated publications

Lorton Communications, P.O. Box 17805, Hillbrow, Johannesburg, South Africa, Tel: 792-2810.
Montfort Press, P.O. Box 5592, Limbe, Tel: 651-883.

Hut accommodation at Mulanje

Principal Forest Officer, P.O. Box 50, Mulanje.

Permits for trout fishing

Nyika – Chelinda Camp
Zomba – Zomba Forestry Office, P.O. Box 29, Zomba, Tel: 523-339
Mulanje – Likhubula Forestry Office, P.O. Box 50, Mulanje, Tel: 465-218.

If you arrive in the forestry reserves after hours and you wish to commence fishing, you may do so after purchasing a permit from the forestry guard on duty.

Zomba Fishing Flies, P.O. Box 313, Zomba, Tel: 522-989.

Service organisations

Rotary Club	P.O. Box 149 Blantyre
	P.O. Box 5091 Limbe
	P.O. Box 53 Lilongwe
Lions	P.O. Box 200 Blantyre
	P.O. Box 30149 Capital City, Lilongwe 3
Round Table	P.O. Box 39 Blantyre
	P.O. Box 433 Lilongwe

Diplomatic representation outside Malawi

Malawi Embassy South Africa	P.O. Box 11172, Brooklyn, Pretoria, South Africa
Malawi High Commission Zimbabwe	42–44 Salisbury Street, Harare, Zimbabwe
Malawi High Commission United Kingdom	33 Grosvenor Street, London, W1X OPE
Malawi Mission to the United Nations	777, 3rd Avenue, New York, New York, 10017
Malawi Embassy Germany	Bunderskanzerplatz, Bonn Centre, H1 1103

Other useful tips

Photography

Even though there may be no notices warning you not to take photographs, do not take photographs in the vicinity of any of the State Residences, near army barracks, government buildings, or in Monkey Bay. If in doubt, always ask for permission to take photographs. Apart from anything else, the dignity of the individual may be offended if you take a photograph without asking for permission.

Politics

As in most other countries, it is considered impolite to discuss politics in public.

CHECKLIST OF COMMON SPECIES

MAMMALS

English name	Latin name
Aardvark	*Orycteropus afer*
Antelope, roan	*Hippotragus equinus*
sable	*Hippotragus niger*
Baboon, yellow	*Papio ursinus*
Buffalo	*Syncerus caffer*
Bushbaby, lesser	*Galago moholi*
Bushbuck	*Tragelaphus scriptus*
Bushpig	*Potamochoerus porcus*
Cheetah	*Acinonyx jubatus*
Civet	*Civettictis civetta*
Dassie	*Dendrohyrax* and *Procavia* spp.
Duiker, blue	*Cephalophus monticolus*
red	*Cephalophus natalensis*
Eland	*Tragelaphus oryx*
Elephant	*Loxodonta africana*
Genet	*Genetta rubiginosa*
Grysbok	*Rhapicerus sharpei*
Hartebeest	*Alcelaphus lichtensteini*
Hippopotamus	*Hippopotamus amphibius*
Honeybadger	*Mellivora capensis*
Hyena	*Crocuta crocuta*
Hyrax, rock	*Dendrohyrax* and *Procavia* spp.
Impala	*Aepyceros melampus*
Jackal, sidestriped	*Canis adustus*
Klipspringer	*Oreotragus oreotragus*
Kudu	*Tragelaphus strepsiceros*
Leopard	*Panthera pardus*

English name	Latin name
Lion	*Panthera leo*
Mongoose, banded	*Mungos mungo*
Monkey, blue	*Cercopithecus albogularis*
vervet	*Cercopithecus pygerythrus*
Nyala	*Tragelaphus angasi*
Otter	*Aonyx capensis*
Porcupine	*Hystrix africaeaustralis*
Reedbuck	*Redunca arundinum*
Rhino, black	*Diceros bicornis*
Serval	*Felis serval*
Squirrel	*Paraxerus cepapi*
Suni, Livingstone's	*Neotragus moschatus*
Warthog	*Phacochoerus aethiopicus*
Waterbuck	*Kobus ellipsiprymnus*
Wild cat	*Felis libyca*
Wild dog	*Lycaon pictus*
Zebra	*Equus burchelli*

BIRDS

English name	Latin name
Akalat, Gunning's	*Sheppardia gunningi*
Sharpe's	*Sheppardia sharpei*
Alethe, Thyolo (Cholo)	*Alethe choloensis*
white-chested	*Alethe fuelleborni*
Apalis, black-headed	*Apalis melanocephala*
white-winged	*Apalis chariessa*
Bee-eater, Boehm's	*Merops boehmi*
carmine	*Merops nubicoides*
little	*Merops pusillus*
Broadbill, African	*Smithornis capensis*
Bunting, Cape	*Emberiza capensis*
Bustard, Denham's	*Otis denhami*
Buzzard, augur	*Buteo rufofuscus*
Chat, mocking	*Thamnolaea cinnamomeiventris*
stone	*Saxicola torquata*

English name	Latin name
Cisticola, churring	*Cisticola njombe*
mountain	*Cisticola hunteri*
rock	*Cisticola aberans*
wailing	*Cisticola lais*
Cormorant, white-breasted	*Phalocrocorax carbo*
Coucal, green	*Ceuthmochares aereus*
Crane, wattled	*Grus carunculatus*
Crow, African pied	*Corvus albus*
Cuckoo, barred, long-tailed	*Cercococcyx montanus*
Dove, cinnamon	*Aplopelia larvata*
Eagle, African fish	*Haliaeetus vocifer*
black	*Aquila verreauxii*
long-crested	*Lophaetus occipitalis*
Egret	*Egretta alba*
Falcon, lanner	*Falco biarmicus*
peregrine	*Falco peregrinus*
Finfoot, African	*Podica senegalensis*
Flycatcher, black-and-white	*Bias musicus*
blue-mantled crested	*Trochocercus cyanomelas*
paradise	*Terpsiphone viridis*
white-tailed, crested	*Trochocercus albonotatus*
Francolin, red-winged	*Francolinus levaillantii crawshayi*
Guinea-fowl, crested	*Guttera edouardi*
Hamerkop	*Scopus umbretta*
Heron, white-backed night	*Gorsachius leuconotus*
Hoopoe, African	*Upupa epops*
Hornbills, crowned	*Bucorvus cafer*
red-billed	*Tockus erythrorhynchus*
yellow-billed	*Tockus flavirostris*
Ibis	*Threskiornis aethiopica*
Jacana	*Actophilornis africanus*
Kingfisher, giant	*Ceryle maxima*
half-collared	*Alcedo semitorquata*
pied	*Ceryle rudis*
Loerie, green	*Tauraco persa*
Livingstone's	*T.P. livingstonii*
Lovebird, Lillian's	*Agapornis lilianae*

English name	Latin name
Mannikin, pied	*Lonchura fringilloides*
Oriole, green-headed	*Oriolus chlorocephalus*
Owl, giant eagle	*Bubo lacteus*
Pel's fishing	*Scotopelia peli*
Pigeon, bronze-naped	*Columba delegorguei*
Pipit, large, striped	*Anthus lineiventris*
Raven, white-necked	*Corvus albicollis*
Robin, olive-flanked	*Cossypha anomala*
red-capped	*Cossypha natalensis*
starred	*Pogonocichla stellata*
Roller, lilac-breasted	*Coracias caudata*
Seedcracker	*Pyrenestes minor*
Seedeater, streaky	*Serinus striolatus*
Shrikes, fiscal	*Lanius collaris*
gorgeous bush	*Malaconotus viridis*
helmet	*Prionops plumata*
Sparrow-weaver, white-browed	*Plocepasser mahali*
Spinetail, mottled	*Telacanthura ussheri*
Starlings, long-tailed	*Lamprotornis mevesii*
Stork, black	*Ciconia nigra*
Sunbird, greater double-collared	*Nectarinia afra whytei*
red-tufted malachite	*Nectarinia johnstoni*
scarlet-chested	*Nectarinia senegalensis*
Swallow, saw-wing	*Psalidoprocne orientalis*
Swift, palm	*Cypsiurus parvus*
Thrush, collared palm	*Cichladusa arquata*
Natal	*Turdus Fischeri*
Trogon, bar-tailed	*Apaloderma vittatum*
Wagtail, long-tailed mountain	*Motacilla clara*
Warbler, red-winged	*Heliolais erythroptera*
Weaver, Bertram's brown-chested	*Ploceus bertrandi*
golden	*Ploceus xanthops*
olive-headed	*Ploceus olivaceiceps*
spotted backed	*Ploceus cucullatus*
yellow	*Ploceus subaureus*

English name	Latin name
Woodpecker, Stierling's	*Dendropicos stierlingi*

REPTILES

English name	Latin name
Crocodile	*Crocodylus niloticus*
Mamba, black	*Dendroaspis polylepis polylepis*
green	*Dendroaspis angusticeps*
Puffadder	*Bitis arietans arietans*

FISH

English name	Latin name
Bass, black	*Mitcropterus salmoides*
Catfish (*kampango*)	*Bagrus meridionalis*
Mbuna (10 genera, over 300 species)	
Mpasa (lake salmon)	*Opsaridium microlepis*
Sanjika	*Opsaridium microcephalus*
Tiger fish	*Hydrocynus vitatus*
Trout, rainbow	*Salmo gairdnerii*
Tsungwa	*Serranochromis robustus*
Vundu	*Heterobranchus longifilis*
Yellowfish	*Barbus johnstonii*

PLANTS

English name	Latin name
Balsam	*Impatiens balsamina*
Begonia	*Begonia* spp.
Blue lobelia	*Lobelia erinus*
Mulanje cedar	*Whydringtonia whyteii*

English name	Latin name
Mulanje iris	*Moraea* spp.
Red-hot poker	*Kniphofia praecox*
Staghorn lily	*Velozia splendens*
Everlasting flower	*Helichrysum* spp.
Whyte's sunflower	*Helichrysum whytenaum*

BIBLIOGRAPHY

Pockets of information about Malawi exist in widely differing sources. This book attempts to draw together material from these sources in such a way that the average tourist to Malawi will have at hand information that might otherwise have taken time and effort to obtain.

Having had their appetite whetted as a result of reading this book, it is hoped that readers who wish to deepen their knowledge will consult the following books – should they be able to obtain them.

Roberts' Birds of Southern Africa, Gordon Lindsay Maclean. John Voelcker Bird Book Fund, 1985.

Cape Maclear, P.A. Cole-King. Publication No 4, Department of Antiquities, Government Press, Zomba, 1978.

British Central Africa – Information for Intending Settlers. First published, London, 1905. Second edition published in 1985 by the Rotary Club of Blantyre.

A Guide to the Fishes of Lake Malawi National Park, Digby Lewis, Peter Reinthal, Jasper Trendall. World Wildlife Fund, Switzerland, 1986.

Malawi – A Guide for Tourists and Businessmen, Mastward Promotions. Blantyre Print and Packaging, 1976.

An Introduction to the Lake Malawi National Park, National Fauna Preservation Society.

Zomba Mountain – A Walker's Guide, H.M. and K.E. Cundy. Montfort Press, 1975.

Birds (pamphlet). Original text by R.J. Dowsett amended 1987 by Michael Gore. Published by SARTOC (Southern African Regional Tourism Council) and Malawi Department of Tourism.

Malawi Orchids (Volume I): Epiphytic Orchids, I. La Croix *et al.* NFPS/SARTOC, 1983.

A Nature Walk in the Heart of Lilongwe: Lilongwe Nature Sanctuary (Pamphlet), Department of National Parks and Wildlife (no date).

The Malawi Collection, D.B. Roy. Malawian Institute of Architects, 1984.

The National Atlas of Malawi, Department of Surveys, 1985.

Guide to the Mulanje Massif, F. Eastwood. Lorton Publications, 1979.

Zomba Plateau and Mulunguzi Nature Trail, National Fauna Preservation Society (3rd edition). Revised 1985.

Lilongwe – An Historical Study, P.A. Cole-King. Publication No 10. Department of Antiquities, Government Press, Zomba, 1971.

Traveller's Health, R. Dawood. Oxford University Press, 1986.

Land of the Lake – A Guide to Malawi, D. Tattersall. Blantyre Periodicals, 1982.

Malawi – Wildlife, Parks and Reserves, J. Carter. Macmillan/The Central Bookshop Ltd, 1987.

Livingstone's Lake, O. Ransford. John Murray/Central Bookshop, 1966.

INDEX

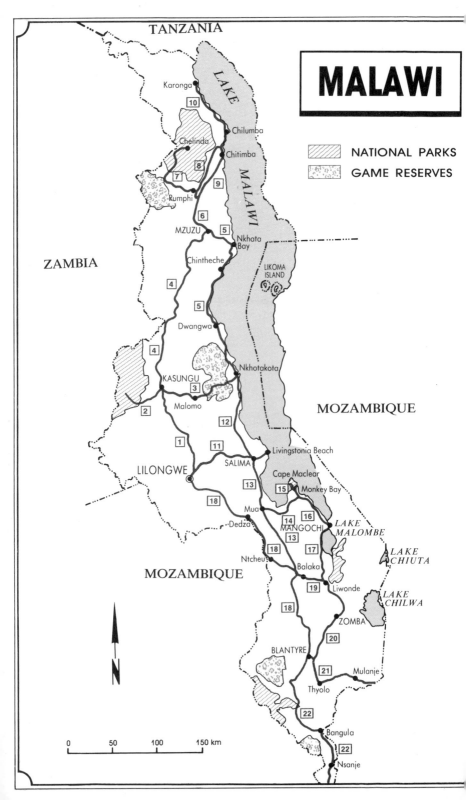